Real

Reading 3

with answers

Liz Driscoll

CAMBRIDGE
UNIVERSITY PRESS

CAMBRIDGE UNIVERSITY PRESS

Cambridge, New York, Melbourne, Madrid, Cape Town, Singapore, São Paulo, Delhi

Cambridge University Press
The Edinburgh Building, Cambridge CB2 8RU, UK

www.cambridge.org
Information on this title: www.cambridge.org/9780521705738

First published 2008

Printed in the United Kingdom at the University Press, Cambridge

A catalogue record for this publication is available from the British Library

ISBN-13 978-0-521-70573-8

Contents

Map of the book

Unit number	Title	Topic	How to ...
1	**I'll cook something**	Cooking and shopping	<ul><li>find information in a text without reading every word</li><li>understand detailed information in a recipe</li><li>choose products from their labels</li><li>understand a till receipt</li></ul>
2	**We've hired a car**	Car hire and driving	<ul><li>search a text for abbreviations and particular words</li><li>find out what car rental payments include</li><li>understand driving laws and road safety advice</li></ul>
3	**Somewhere to live**	Finding accommodation	<ul><li>put yourself in the position of someone reading advertisements in the real world</li><li>understand advertisements for rented accommodation</li><li>work out the meaning of abbreviations</li><li>understand a tenancy agreement</li></ul>
4	**I'll check it in**	Taking luggage on a plane	<ul><li>skim a webpage to get a general idea of what it is about</li><li>find out how much checked baggage you can take on a plane</li><li>fill in a form about delayed luggage</li></ul>
5	**I'll be at home**	Dealing with mail	<ul><li>use a variety of skills when reading texts</li><li>follow instructions about having your mail redelivered</li><li>follow instructions about having your water supply interrupted</li></ul>
6	**A weekend in Wales**	Booking holiday accommodation	<ul><li>relate information you already know to what you read in a text</li><li>understand a description of bed and breakfast accommodation</li><li>understand a letter of confirmation and the rules about cancelled accommodation</li></ul>
7	**I saw an article about it**	Magazine articles	<ul><li>identify the main point in a paragraph</li><li>identify a dramatic beginning to an article</li><li>follow the order of events in a narrative</li></ul>
8	**In the newspapers**	Newspapers	<ul><li>identify newspaper sections and articles from these sections</li><li>read a newspaper selectively</li><li>find the main points in a newspaper article</li></ul>

Social and Travel

Unit number	Title	Topic	How to ...
9	**Safety at work**	Fire regulations	o work out the meaning of unknown words from the context o understand a leaflet about preventing a fire o follow instructions for a fire drill
10	**Lines of communication**	Emails and notices at work	o work out who an email is from and who it is to o work out the main purpose of an email o understand resignation and appointment notices
11	**Any comments?**	Questionnaires and feedback	o interpret a completed questionnaire o distinguish between comments and suggested action o understand how writers link facts and ideas
12	**I'm going to apply**	Job applications	o understand a job advertisement o distinguish between formal and informal language o understand an offer of employment and confirm acceptance
13	**I'm off on a trip**	Business travel research	o interpret statistics o interpret charts and graphs o find out about business etiquette in another country
14	**Look it up!**	Using reference materials	o find information in a reference book o use reference books to complete a crossword o find answers to questions in a reference book
15	**It's on the shelf**	Using a library database	o understand instructions in a library catalogue o understand what a novel is about from the blurb o read fiction without worrying about difficult language
16	**Read about reading**	The process of reading	o skim a text and identify the main points o identify the topic of each paragraph within a text o relate what you have read to your own experiences

Work and Study

I would particularly like to thank Ros Henderson, of Cambridge University Press, for her support and guidance in the writing of this book, as well as for her superb editing. I am also very grateful to Brigit Viney for her wonderful comments and suggestions, to Nóirín Burke, who commissioned the project, and to Linda Matthews for overseeing its production.

My thanks go to Stephanie White and Paul Fellows at Kamae Design for their creative design work.

I am also grateful to Bill Henman, Ian Lees, Marcos Martos Higueras, Jane Read, Marina Rose, Richard Walker and Mary Yoe for their help in finding the texts.

The author and publishers are grateful to the following reviewers for their valuable insights and suggestions:

Steve Banfield, United Arab Emirates; Ildiko Berke, Hungary; Ian Chisholm, UK; Alper Darici, Turkey; Helen Dixon, UK; Rosie Ganne, UK; Jean Greenwood, UK; Elif Isler, Turkey; Kathy Kolarik, Australia; L. Krishnaveni, Malaysia; Beatriz Martín, Spain; Steve Miller, UK; Ersoy Osman, UK

The authors and publishers acknowledge the following sources of copyright material and are grateful for the permissions granted. While every effort has been made, it has not always been possible to identify the sources of all the material used, or to trace all copyright holders. If any omissions are brought to our notice, we will be happy to include the appropriate acknowledgements on reprinting.

pp. 10–11: National Magazine Company for recipe 'Pasta with aubergine and mozzarella sauce' from *Good Housekeeping Complete Book of Pasta;* pp. 14–16: Avis for the car rental voucher and material from their website, © 2000–2007 AVIS Rent A Car; pp. 22–23: Air Canada for webpages, checked baggage allowance and excess baggage fees, www.aircanada.com; pp. 26–27: Royal Mail 'Sorry, you were out' card and 'Making Redelivery easy' text from www.royalmail.com Reproduced by kind permission of Royal Mail Group Ltd. All Rights Reserved.; p. 28: Thames Water for 'Interruptions to your water supply' card, © 2007 Thames Water Utilities; pp. 31–33: Ceri and Elaine Morgan for Ramsey House letter and website material from www.stayinwales.co.uk; p. 35: article 'Call of the Wild' from *Horizons The Magazine of Explore!*, June 2006, by permission of Sandy Beatty of Explore! (www.explore.co.uk); pp. 36–37: *Getaway* magazine for the article 'A walk in the park', August 2004; p. 39: *The Times* for article by Jeremy Whittle, 'Cooke shows ingredients for big prize', 20 September 2006, © N I Syndication; p. 39: article 'Cyclists facing £2,500 bell fines' by Tim Shipman, *Daily Mail*, 11 September 2006 and p. 40: 'Cyclists with helmets "more like to be hit"' by Ray Massey, *Daily Mail*, 12 September 2006 © Associated Newspapers Ltd; p. 39: article 'The bicycle that turned into folding money' by Ben Laurance, *Observer*, 7 August 2005; p. 43: text from Excess Baggage brochure, Excess Baggage Group Ltd; p. 43: Southern Electric 'call- back' card, © Scottish and Southern Energy Group; p. 44: Merricks Media Ltd for text 'New beginning' by Amanda Hemmings, *Australia and New Zealand*, August and September 2006; p. 47: The Midcounties Co-operative for text 'Help prevent fire' and p. 81: 'Slips, trips and falls are a danger to you and your customers', Scriptographic Publications Ltd; p. 48: Cambridge University Press for fire drill procedure; pp. 66–67: for entries for

'brass', 'lycra', 'metal' from *Cambridge Advanced Learner's Dictionary, 2nd Edition*, 2005; pp. 66–67: entries for 'ground' and 'mental' from *Cambridge Idioms Dictionary, 2nd Edition*, 2006; p. 70: entry for 'fiction' and pp. 92–95: all entries from *Cambridge Learner's Dictionary, 3rd Edition*, 2004, © Cambridge University Press, reproduced with permission; pp. 66–67: entries for 'follower' and 'stare' from *Penguin Reference Pocket Thesaurus*, edited by Rosalind Fergusson, Martin Manser and David Pickering, Penguin Books, 2004, © Penguin Group UK; pp. 66–67: definitions 'Laurel and Hardy', 'Channel Islands' and 'insect' from *Hutchinson Encyclopedia*, 2001, Helicon, RM Education plc; pp. 68–69: extracts from the *Chambers Book of Facts*, © Chambers 2005. Reproduced by permission of Chambers Harrap Publishers Ltd; pp. 70–71: Oxfordshire County Council for adapted text 'Library Catalogue Help', www.libcat.oxfordshire.gov.uk; p. 73: text from *4.50 from Paddington* by Agatha Christie, and p. 79: extract from *Death on the Nile* by Agatha Christie, published by HarperCollins, © Agatha Christie Ltd; pp. 74–76: text 'Reading' excerpted from *The World Book Encyclopedia*, © 2007. By permission of the publisher: www.worldbookonline.com; p. 79: extract 'Wanted: a computer, female aged 18–25' from *Much Ado About English: Up and Down the Bizarre Byways of a Fascinating Language* by Richard Watson Todd, Nicholas Brealey Publishing; p. 79: tables 'Watches and clocks: exports 2002–2005' and 'Watches and clocks: imports 2002–2005', © International Trade Centre, 2007; p. 81: Usdaw for texts 'Should first aid be provided in my workplace?' and 'Can my employer stop me putting entries into the accident book?' from www.usdaw.org.uk

The publishers are grateful to the following for permission to reproduce copyright photographs and material:

Key: l = left, c = centre, r = right, t = top, b = bottom

Alamy/©Andrew Butterton for p. 26 /©Afripics.com for p. 36 /©Louise Murray for p. 37 /©Photofusion Picture Library for p. 40 /©A M Corporation for p. 54 /©Asia Images Group for p. 64 /©Ian Shaw for p. 74 (t) /©Kitt Cooper-Smith for p. 77; Britain on View for p. 30; Corbis Images/©Jon Hicks for p. 14; News International Syndication for p. 39 (l); Photolibrary/©PhotoDisc for p. 35; Punchstock/©Image Source for p. 33 /©Bananastock for p. 50 /©Digital Vision for p. 58 /©Comstock for p. 71 /©Image Source for p. 74 (b); Shutterstock/©TT Photo for p. 39 (r); Tourism Australia /©Nino Ellison for p. 44.

Front cover of *The Penguin Reference Pocket Thesaurus* edited by Rosalind Fergusson, Martin Manser and David Pickering (Penguin Books, 2004) on p. 66 (3) copyright ©Penguin Books Ltd, 2004.

Front cover of *The Hutchinson Concise Encyclopaedia* on p. 66 (2) Copyright © RM Education plc.

Cover of *4.50 From Paddington* on p. 72 ©1957 Agatha Christie Limited, a Chorion company, all rights reserved.

Illustrations:

Kathy Baxendale pp. 29, 30, 40, 62, 63; Mark Duffin pp. 11, 12, 23, 24, 25, 43, 46, 52, 65; Laura Martinez p. 19; Rory Walker p. 22.

Text design and page make-up: Kamae Design, Oxford
Cover design: Kamae Design, Oxford
Cover photo: © Getty Images
Picture research: Hilary Luckcock

Introduction
To the student

Who is *Real Reading 3* for?

You can use this book if you are a student at intermediate or upper-intermediate level and you want to improve your English reading. You can use the book alone without a teacher or you can use it in a classroom with a teacher.

How will *Real Reading 3* help me with my reading?

Real Reading 3 contains texts for everyday reading practice, for example leaflets, notices, websites, newspapers, etc. It is designed to help you with reading you will need to do in English at home or when visiting another country.

The exercises in each unit help you develop useful skills such as working out the meaning of unknown words from context and ignoring parts of the text which are not useful to you. *Real Reading 3* discourages you from using a dictionary to find out the meaning of every word you do not know.

How is *Real Reading 3* organized?

The book has 16 units and is divided into two sections:
- Units 1–8 – social and travel situations
- Units 9–16 – work and study situations

Every unit is divided into Reading A and Reading B and has:
- *Get ready to read*: to introduce you to the topic of the unit
- *Learning tip*: to help you improve your learning
- *Class bonus*: an exercise you can do with other students or friends
- *Focus on*: to help you study useful grammar or vocabulary
- *Did you know?*: extra information about vocabulary, different cultures or the topic of the unit
- *Extra practice*: an extra exercise for more practice
- *Can-do checklist*: to help you think about what you learnt in the unit.

After each section there is a review unit. The reviews help you practise the skills you learn in each section.

At the back of the book you can find:
- *Appendices*: contain lists of *Useful language*, *Learning tips* for every unit and information about *Using a dictionary*.
- *Answer key*: gives correct answers and possible answers for exercises that have more than one answer.

How can I use *Real Reading 3*?

The units at the end of the book are more difficult than the units at the beginning of the book. However, you do not need to do the units in order. It is better to choose the units that are most interesting for you and to do them in the order you prefer.

There are many different ways you can use this book. We suggest you work in this way:
- Look in the *Contents* list and find a unit that interests you.
- Prepare yourself for reading by working through the *Get ready to read* exercises.
- Look at *Appendix 1: Useful language* for the unit.
- Do the exercises in Reading A. Use the example answers to guide you. Put the *Learning tip* into practice (either in Reading A or Reading B).
- Do the exercises in Reading B.
- Check your answers either with your teacher or with the *Answer Key*.
- If you want to do more work, do the *Extra practice* activity.
- At the end of the unit, think about what you have learnt and complete the *Can-do checklist*.
- Look at the list of *Learning tips* in *Appendix 2* and decide which other tips you have used in the unit.

What is *Cambridge English Skills*?

Real Reading 3 is one of 12 books in the *Cambridge English Skills* series. The series also contains *Real Writing* and *Real Listening & Speaking* books and offers skills training to students from elementary to advanced level. All the books are available in with-answers and without-answers editions.

Level	Book	Author
Elementary CEF: A2 Cambridge ESOL: KET NQF Skills for life: Entry 2	Real Reading 1 with answers	Liz Driscoll
	Real Reading 1 without answers	Liz Driscoll
	Real Writing 1 with answers and audio CD	Graham Palmer
	Real Writing 1 without answers	Graham Palmer
	Real Listening & Speaking 1 with answers and audio CDs (2)	Miles Craven
	Real Listening & Speaking 1 without answers	Miles Craven
Pre-intermediate CEF: B1 Cambridge ESOL: PET NQF Skills for life: Entry 3	Real Reading 2 with answers	Liz Driscoll
	Real Reading 2 without answers	Liz Driscoll
	Real Writing 2 with answers and audio CD	Graham Palmer
	Real Writing 2 without answers	Graham Palmer
	Real Listening & Speaking 2 with answers and audio CDs (2)	Sally Logan & Craig Thaine
	Real Listening & Speaking 2 without answers	Sally Logan & Craig Thaine
Intermediate to upper-intermediate CEF: B2 Cambridge ESOL: FCE NQF Skills for life: Level 1	Real Reading 3 with answers	Liz Driscoll
	Real Reading 3 without answers	Liz Driscoll
	Real Writing 3 with answers and audio CD	Roger Gower
	Real Writing 3 without answers	Roger Gower
	Real Listening & Speaking 3 with answers and audio CDs (2)	Miles Craven
	Real Listening & Speaking 3 without answers	Miles Craven
Advanced CEF: C1 Cambridge ESOL: CAE NQF Skills for life: Level 2	Real Reading 4 with answers	Liz Driscoll
	Real Reading 4 without answers	Liz Driscoll
	Real Writing 4 with answers and audio CD	Simon Haines
	Real Writing 4 without answers	Simon Haines
	Real Listening & Speaking 4 with answers and audio CDs (2)	Miles Craven
	Real Listening & Speaking 4 without answers	Miles Craven

Where are the teacher's notes?

The series is accompanied by a dedicated website containing detailed teaching notes and extension ideas for every unit of every book. Please visit www.cambridge.org/englishskills to access the *Cambridge English Skills* teacher's notes.

What are the main aims of *Real Reading 3*?

- To help students develop reading skills in accordance with the ALTE (Association of Language Testers in Europe) Can-do statements. These statements describe what language users can typically do at different levels and in different contexts. Visit www.alte.org for further information.
- To encourage autonomous learning by focusing on learner training.

What are the key features of *Real Reading 3*?

- It is aimed at intermediate and upper-intermediate learners of English at levels B1–B2 of the Council of Europe's CEFR (Common European Framework of Reference for Languages).
- It contains 16 four-page units, divided into two sections: Social and Travel, and Work and Study.
- *Real Reading 3* units are divided into Reading A and Reading B and contain:
  - *Get ready to read* warm-up exercises to get students thinking about the topic
  - *Learning tips* which give students advice on how to improve their reading and their learning
  - *Class bonus* communication activities for pairwork and group work so that you can adapt the material to suit your class
  - *Focus on* exercises which provide contextualized practice in particular language or vocabulary areas
  - *Did you know?* boxes which provide notes on cultural or linguistic differences between English-speaking countries, or factual information on the topic of the unit
  - *Extra practice* extension tasks which provide more real world reading practice
  - *Can-do checklists* at the end of every unit to encourage students to think about what they have learnt.
- There are two review units to practise skills that have been introduced in the units.
- It has an international feel and contains a range of texts from English-speaking countries.
- It can be used as self-study material, in class, or as supplementary homework material.

What is the best way to use *Real Reading 3* in the classroom?

The book is designed so that the units may be used in any order, although the more difficult units naturally appear near the end of the book, in the *Work and Study* section.

You can consult the unit-by-unit teacher's notes at www.cambridge.org/englishskills for detailed teaching ideas. However, broadly speaking, different parts of the book can be approached in the following ways:

- *Useful language*: You can use the *Useful language* lists in *Appendix 1* to preteach or revise the vocabulary from the unit you are working on.
- *Get ready to read*: It is a good idea to use this section as an introduction to the topic. Students can work on the exercises in pairs or groups. Many of these require students to answer questions about their personal experience. These questions can be used as prompts for discussion. Some exercises contain a problem-solving element that students can work on together. Other exercises aim to clarify key vocabulary in the unit. You can present these vocabulary items directly to students.
- *Learning tips*: You can ask students to read and discuss these in an open-class situation. An alternative approach is for you to create a series of discussion questions associated with the *Learning tip*. Students can discuss their ideas in pairs or small groups followed by open-class feedback. The *Learning tip* acts as a reflective learning tool to help promote learner autonomy.
- *Class bonuses*: The material in these activities aims to provide freer practice. You can set these up carefully, then take the role of observer during the activity so that students carry out the task freely. You can make yourself available to help students or analyze the language they produce during the activity.
- *Extra practice*: These activities can be set as homework or out-of-class projects for your students. Alternatively, students can do some activities in pairs during class time.
- *Can-do checklists*: Refer to these at the beginning of a lesson to explain to students what the lesson will cover, and again at the end so that students can evaluate their learning for themselves.
- *Appendices*: You may find it useful to refer your students to the *Useful language*, *Learning tips* and *Using a dictionary* sections. Students can use these as general checklists to help them with their reading.

Unit 1
I'll cook something

Get ready to read

- Circle the words in these sentences so that they are true for you.
  I prefer to buy *locally produced / organic / cheap* food.
  I usually buy *fresh / ready-made / frozen* food.
  I usually do my shopping *in a supermarket / at a market / online*.
  I *never / hardly ever / often* cook for friends.
  I like trying new recipes from *my own country / my own and one or two other countries / all over the world*.

- Match the beginnings and endings of these sentences.
  a Bolognese sauce   is made from peanut butter, garlic, vinegar and chilli peppers.
  b Béchamel sauce   is made from sugar, soy sauce and rice vinegar.
  c Satay sauce   is made from minced beef, carrot and tomato puree.
  d Sweet and sour sauce   is made from flour, butter and milk.

- Do you know where each of the sauces above comes from?

go to Useful language p. 82

A What should I make?

1 You want to cook for some friends and decide to compare some recipes. Look at these three sets of ingredients and find a pasta dish that uses tinned tomatoes, garlic and Parmesan cheese. (You like this combination of flavours.)

Pasta with aubergine and green pepper sauce

(SERVES 4)

1 large aubergine, diced
1 onion, chopped
2 tbsp olive oil
1 garlic clove, crushed
1 green pepper, de-seeded and chopped
1 tbsp fresh basil
225 g tomatoes, skinned and chopped
salt and black pepper
400 g pasta
4 tbsp freshly grated Parmesan cheese

Pasta with fresh tomato and olive sauce

(serves 4)

4 large ripe tomatoes

125 g stoned black Greek-style olives, roughly chopped

2 garlic cloves, peeled and finely chopped

4 tbsp fresh basil, chopped

150 ml olive oil

salt and black pepper

400 g pasta

Pasta with aubergine and mozzarella sauce

(serves 4)

90 ml olive oil
1 onion, peeled and chopped
2 garlic cloves, peeled and crushed
1 medium aubergine, about 400 g, diced
400 g can chopped tomatoes
salt and black pepper
15 g fresh basil leaves, shredded
150 g mozzarella cheese, diced
2 tbsp pine nuts
4 tbsp freshly grated Parmesan cheese
400 g pasta

ml = millilitre   g = gram   tsp = teaspoon   tbsp = tablespoon

Focus on ...
verbs

ab**C**def

Look at the pictures. Circle the correct word in each pair.

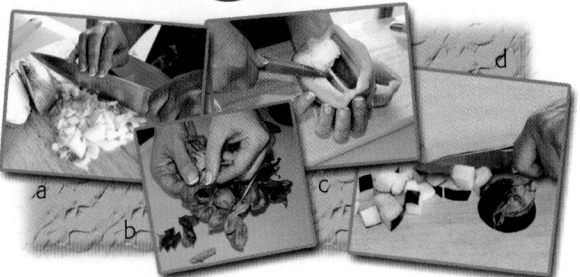

a stone / chop
b peel / shred
c crush / de-seed
d dice / grate

Match these pictures with the verbs you did not use.

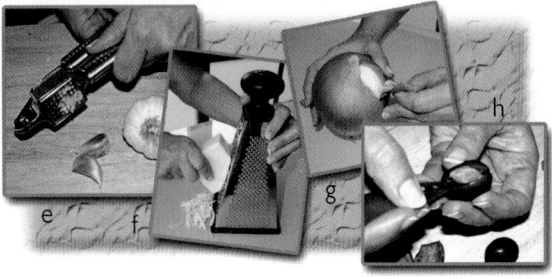

e ....
f ....
g ....
h ....

2 You already have olive oil, garlic and pine nuts. What else do you need to make the pasta dish you chose in Exercise 1? Make a list.

....
....
....

3 Read the instructions for making the dish you chose in Exercise 1. Are the statements below true (T) or false (F)?

1 Fry the onion, garlic and aubergine for 8–10 minutes in the olive oil.
2 Add the tomatoes and seasoning. Bring to the boil, lower the heat and simmer for 15 minutes.
3 Meanwhile, cook the pasta in plenty of salted water until *al dente*.
4 Drain the pasta, and mix with the tomato and aubergine sauce. Add the basil, mozzarella and pine nuts, and mix well.
5 Serve at once, with the Parmesan handed out separately.

a You fry the aubergine. ..T..
b You cook the pasta at the same time as the sauce. ......
c You need to use the mozzarella before the tomatoes. ......
d You add the Parmesan before serving. ......
e You need to cook the pine nuts before you add them to the pasta. ......

4 You want to make an Italian dessert to go with your pasta dish. A friend has given you this recipe for tiramisù. Read it and add the ingredients you need to the shopping list.

Tiramisù
1 Cover bottom of dish with sponge fingers (about 15). Soak with strong fresh coffee.
2 Separate 3 eggs. Beat egg whites until firm.
3 Mix 250 g mascarpone into egg whites.
4 Add egg yolks and 2 tbsp sugar, and mix. Pour over sponge fingers.
5 Sieve 1 tsp cocoa powder over mixture.
6 Cover and leave in fridge overnight before serving.

DON'T FORGET TO BUY

sponge fingers (about 15)
....
....
....
....
....

Did you know ...?

Tiramisù is an Italian dish and its name means 'pick me up'. The dessert could be a *pick-me-up* – something which will make you feel better. Or perhaps you will need someone to *pick you up* – lift you – after you have eaten it because it is so rich.

B Which one should I buy?

1 You are going to make pasta with aubergine and mozzarella sauce and tiramisù for three friends. Look again at the lists of ingredients you made in Exercises 2 and 4 on page 11.

2 You are in the supermarket choosing the ingredients you need. Look quickly at the labels on these pages and decide which dish each pair of products is for.

Pasta with aubergine and mozzarella sauce 1a and 1b

Tiramisù _____

1a

69p
egg penne
delicious fresh egg pasta
Cooking time 3 MINUTES
Display until 05 JUL
Use by 07 JULY
250 g

1b

high in fibre
59p
wholewheat penne
made from 100% durum wheat
Store in a cool place.
Allow 50 - 75g of pasta per person for a starter, 75 - 100g for a main course.
Add salt and simmer for 10 - 12 minutes.
500 g

2a

DISPLAY UNTIL 23 JUNE
BEST BEFORE 30 JUNE
86p
HEDGEROW FARM
6 large barn eggs
laid by hens in large barns

2b

6 eggs from hens which are free to roam outdoors and whose diet contains grains which are not genetically modified
MEDIUM
DISPLAY UNTIL 20 JUNE
BEST BEFORE 27 JUNE
89p
L

3a

35 g
Black Peppercorns
Use whole or grind in a pepper mill
£1.38

3b

£1.55
Ground Black Pepper
Ideal for savoury dishes
33 g

4a

£2.11
Extra mature Parmesan From Italy
Fresh grated Parmigiano Reggiano
Full Flavour
120 gram

4b

Grated Italian
Suitable for all pasta dishes
Hard Cheese
partially dried Italian hard cheese
99p
80 gram

5a

Keep it fresh easy resealable pack
Colombian
Coffee beans
for grinding medium roasted suitable for all machines
227 gram e
£2.25

5b

10 cup - size
Coffee filters
£1.95
ground coffee medium
How to serve
Shake the filter and rest it on the cup.
Pour in freshly boiled water and leave for 3 - 4 minutes.

6a

58p Italian
PLUM TOMATOES
in tasty tomato juice
400 g

6b

Quality CHOPPED TOMATOES
A new packaging
This carton is safe and light, and easy to open, pour and store
45p
390 gram

3 Look again at the product labels and think about the advantages and disadvantages of each item in each pair. Use a chart to make notes about cost, quality, preparation time and equipment needed.

	Ingredient	Advantages	Disadvantages
1a	egg penne	cooks in 3 minutes	expensive, packet too small for 4 people
1b	wholewheat penne	healthier, cheaper, bigger packet	takes longer to cook
2a			
2b etc.			

4 Now decide which product from each pair you are going to buy. What are your reasons?

Class bonus

Work in small groups. Discuss your choices. Have you chosen the same products?

5 Look at the till receipt below. Did you choose the same products as this shopper?

```
QUAL CHPPD TOM                           £0.45
CASTER SUGAR                             £0.59
SPONGE FINGER                            £0.79
WHOLEWHEAT PENNE                         £0.59
MEDIUM EGGS X6                           £0.89
GRD B/PEPPR                              £1.55
COCOA                                    £2.29
GRATED PARMESAN                          £2.11
ROCKET SALAD                             £1.64
DRY BLK OLIVES                           £1.05
MOZZARELLA BAG                           £1.09
AUBERGINE                                £0.99
BUNCH BASIL                              £0.75
ONIONS LOOSE 0.3 KG @ 0.73/KG            £0.22
COFFEE FILTER                            £1.95
TABLE SALT BOTTLE                        £0.30
ORGANIC BREAD                            £1.35
FRUIT JUICE 1L            2 @ £1.99
                                         £3.98

BALANCE DUE                             £22.58
CASH                                    £30.00
CHANGE DUE                               £7.42
```

6 What else did this shopper buy in order to make pasta with aubergine and mozzarella sauce and tiramisù? Circle the purchases on the till receipt.

E X tra practice

Have a look in your kitchen cupboards at home. Have any of the packets got ingredients or instructions in English? The next time you go shopping, buy something with instructions in English. Try and follow the English instructions when you use the ingredients.

Can-do checklist

Tick what you can do.

	Can do	Need more practice
I can find information in a text without reading every word.		
I can understand detailed information in a recipe.		
I can choose products from their labels.		
I can understand a till receipt.		

Unit 2
We've hired a car

go to Useful language p. 82

Get ready to read

- How do people usually travel around when they visit your country on holiday?
  Tick ✓ one or more of the boxes.
  boat ☐   bus ☐   car ☐   plane ☐   train ☐

- Add *never* to these sentences where necessary to make them true for you.
  I've .... been abroad on holiday.
  I've .... flown to a holiday destination.
  I've .... driven a hire car on holiday.
  I've .... collected a hire car from the airport.

- In this unit, you are going to read about two people who are going to South Africa on holiday. Which of these cities are in South Africa? Tick ✓ one or more of the boxes.
  Abuja ☐   Cape Town ☐   Durban ☐   Johannesburg ☐   Nairobi ☐

A Terms and conditions

1 Claudio and Flavia Martinuzzo are going on holiday to South Africa. They have arranged car hire with Avis and have received the car rental voucher below. Look at the voucher and (circle) the cities to make a correct sentence.

They are collecting the car from *Cape Town / Durban / Johannesburg* and they are returning it to *Cape Town / Durban / Johannesburg*.

AVIS CAR RENTAL VOUCHER

RENTER'S NAME MR C MARTINUZZO	ISSUED BY
VOUCHER NUMBER 3729656-0	DATE ISSUED 11 JUL
RENTAL LOCATION CPT DOWNTOWN	RESERVATION NUMBER 39073636GB0
RENTAL DATE 30 AUG RENTAL LENGTH 20 days	CAR GROUP - CODE B BILLING INFORMATION
RETURN LOCATION JNB AIRPORT	TOUR CODE No
REMARKS INCL: CDW/PAI/TLW/UM/TAX/SURCHARGE	

Learning tip

We sometimes search a text for a specific piece of information – this could be the answer to a question or simply a particular word or words. This type of reading is called scanning. When we scan, we do not read every word. We look quickly to find what we are looking for. Scanning may be the first step in our reading of a text. Once we have found something we are looking for, we might go on to read the text around it.

---

2 Claudio and Flavia had to pay more because they arranged a one-way rental. Read this part of the Terms and Conditions on the Avis South Africa website. How much more did they have to pay? Tick ✓ one of the boxes.

a ZAR 123.12 ☐
b ZAR 264.24 ☐
c ZAR 406.98 ☐
d ZAR 615.60 ☐

3 Look again at the *Remarks* section of the rental voucher. How many extras have Claudio and Flavia paid for? Write a list.

4 Claudio and Flavia look for explanations of these extras in this other part of the Terms and Conditions. Scan the webpage on the right and answer these questions.

a Which extras on the rental voucher are explained?

----

b What do the abbreviations stand for?

----

c Can you guess the meaning of any abbreviations that are not explained?

----

5 Look at the Surcharges and Tax. Underline the charges that Claudio and Flavia have to pay.

6 Claudio and Flavia have chosen Limited Cover accident insurance (CDW). If they have an accident, will they pay more or less than if they had chosen SCDW?

7 Would you choose Limited Cover or Super Cover for accidents and theft? Why?

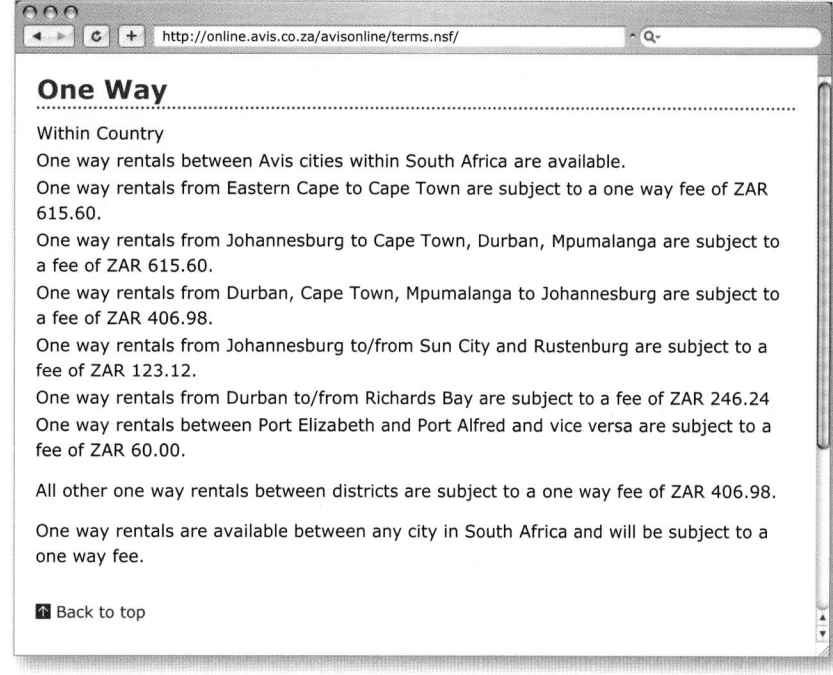

http://online.avis.co.za/avisonline/terms.nsf/

One Way

Within Country
One way rentals between Avis cities within South Africa are available.
One way rentals from Eastern Cape to Cape Town are subject to a one way fee of ZAR 615.60.
One way rentals from Johannesburg to Cape Town, Durban, Mpumalanga are subject to a fee of ZAR 615.60.
One way rentals from Durban, Cape Town, Mpumalanga to Johannesburg are subject to a fee of ZAR 406.98.
One way rentals from Johannesburg to/from Sun City and Rustenburg are subject to a fee of ZAR 123.12.
One way rentals from Durban to/from Richards Bay are subject to a fee of ZAR 246.24
One way rentals between Port Elizabeth and Port Alfred and vice versa are subject to a fee of ZAR 60.00.

All other one way rentals between districts are subject to a one way fee of ZAR 406.98.

One way rentals are available between any city in South Africa and will be subject to a one way fee.

⬆ Back to top

ZAR = South African Rands

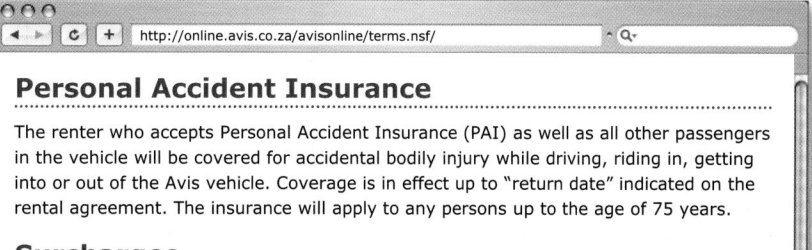

http://online.avis.co.za/avisonline/terms.nsf/

Personal Accident Insurance

The renter who accepts Personal Accident Insurance (PAI) as well as all other passengers in the vehicle will be covered for accidental bodily injury while driving, riding in, getting into or out of the Avis vehicle. Coverage is in effect up to "return date" indicated on the rental agreement. The insurance will apply to any persons up to the age of 75 years.

Surcharges

- 9% Airport surcharge is applicable on all rentals from an airport location.
- 1% Tourism levy is applicable on all rentals at all locations.
- A rental contract fee of ZAR 30.78 is applicable on all rentals.

Tax

14% VAT applicable.

Waivers

COLLISION DAMAGE WAIVER (CDW)
Avis offers you the choice of two optional Collision Damage Waiver Insurances.
Option 1 – Collision Damage Waiver (CDW) Limited Cover
Choosing this option means that in the event of an accident, the renter is responsible for up to a specified amount for damage repair.
Option 2 – Super Cover Collision Damage Waiver (SCDW) Super Cover
This option means that the renter will be liable for a reduced excess which lowers the responsibility of the renter for payment arising from collision damage caused to the vehicle or part thereof.
THEFT LOSS WAIVER
Avis offers you the choice of two optional Theft Loss Waiver Insurances.
Option 1 – Theft Loss Waiver (TLW) Limited Cover
Choosing this option means that in the event of theft of a vehicle or part thereof, the renter is responsible for up to a specified amount for the replacement of the applicable loss by theft. Personal property is not covered.
Option 2 – Super Theft Loss Waiver (STLW) Super Cover
This option means that the renter will be liable for a reduced excess which lowers the responsibility of the renter for payment arising from theft of a vehicle or part thereof. Personal property is not covered.

B Safe driving in South Africa

1 Claudio and Flavia arrive in Cape Town and go to Avis to collect their car. The rental agent gives them the envelope on the right which contains the rental agreement. Should they keep the envelope until the end of their trip?

Did you know ...?

In most countries, vehicles are driven on the right-hand side of the road. However, in some countries, such as Australia, India, Indonesia, Ireland, Japan, Malaysia, New Zealand, Thailand, the UK and South Africa, vehicles are driven on the left-hand side.

In most countries, speed and distances are measured in kilometres. In the UK and the USA, however, speed and distances are measured in miles. There are approximately 1.6 kilometres to the mile.

2 The agent tells Claudio and Flavia that they always need to carry cash when driving. Read the information on the envelope and find out why. Complete what the rental agent tells them.

> You'll need to carry cash because _____
> _____
> _____

KINDLY INDICATE YOUR RETURN KM READING, FUEL GAUGE READING, DATE AND TIME, AND RETURN THIS ENVELOPE, WITH YOUR KEYS, TO THE RENTAL COUNTER.

DOCUMENT NUMBER ☐☐☐☐☐☐☐☐

RETURN KM READING										
RETURN FUEL GAUGE ✓	E	$\frac{1}{8}$	$\frac{1}{4}$	$\frac{3}{8}$	$\frac{1}{2}$	$\frac{5}{8}$	$\frac{3}{4}$	$\frac{7}{8}$	F	

RETURN DATE	RETURN TIME

Safe Driving in South Africa

DRIVER'S LICENCE
When driving, you must be in possession of your driver's licence at all times.

SEAT BELTS
The law requires that you wear seat belts at all times.

DRIVING
In South Africa, driving is on the left-hand side of the road.

SPEED LIMITS
Generally 60 km/hr in built-up areas, 100 km/hr in rural areas and 120 km/hr on highways.

PETROL
Petrol is available 24 hours per day. Unleaded petrol should be used in Avis cars. Credit cards are not accepted for the payment of petrol.

SAFETY
For your own safety, keep your doors locked while driving.

LOCK UP
Shut windows and lock all doors and the boot when leaving the vehicle unattended.

VALUABLES
Do not leave personal belongings such as cell phones and valuables in your vehicle. They are not covered by our insurance.

TYRES
Avis undertakes that on delivery of the vehicle to the renter, the condition of the tyres will be in compliance with legislation and the tyre pressure in accordance with the vehicle manufacturer's specification for 'normal use'.

It is the responsibility of the renter to ensure that both the condition and inflation of the tyres are appropriate throughout the course of the rental.

It is the responsibility of the renter to inspect the condition of the tyres at commencement of the rental and to make adjustments to the tyre pressure to take into account such factors as the number of passengers, mass of luggage, ambient temperatures, speed and road condition.

IMMOBILISER
Please use the immobiliser when leaving the vehicle unattended.

ROAD MAPS
Maps of Southern Africa, including city and regional maps, can be found in a copy of the Avis Inbound magazine, in each vehicle or at the Avis Customer Service Centre. More extensive area maps are obtainable from the Automobile Association (AA) and South African Tourism.

Avis Careline: +27 (0)800 001 669
24 hour breakdown and medical emergencies

Avis Central Reservations:
National: +27 (0)861 021 111
International: +27 (0)861 034 444
Preferred Service: +27 (0)861 113 333
Website: www.avis.co.za

Avis rents Volkswagen and other fine cars.

AVIS
We try harder.

3 Claudio and Flavia don't want to break the law when they are driving in South Africa. What four things do they have to do to stay within the law? Complete what Flavia tells Claudio.

a We have to carry our driving licences all the time.

b We _____

c We _____

d We _____

4 What four pieces of advice does the information on the envelope give? Complete what Claudio tells Flavia.

a We should keep our doors locked while driving.

b We _____

c We _____

d We _____

5 Which part of the car should Claudio and Flavia check regularly?

_____

6 Which telephone number on the envelope is probably the most useful for Claudio and Flavia while they are in South Africa? Why?

_____

Focus on ...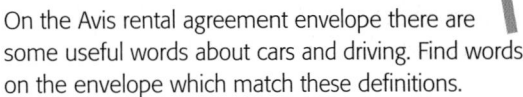
vocabulary

On the Avis rental agreement envelope there are some useful words about cars and driving. Find words on the envelope which match these definitions.

a a closed space at the back of a car for storing things
  b o o t

b something such as a car or bus that takes people from one place to another, especially using roads
  _ _ _ _ _ _ _ _

c a thick, round piece of rubber filled with air, that fits around a wheel _ _ _ _

d a device fitted to a car which stops it from moving so that it cannot be stolen _ _ _ _ _ _ _ _ _ _ _

Compound nouns are nouns which consist of two words. Find compound nouns on the envelope which match these definitions.

e a piece of equipment that you use to measure how much petrol you have used _ _ _ _ _ _ _ _ _ _

f an official document that allows you to drive a car
  _ _ _ _ _ _ _ _ _ _ _ _ _ _ _

g a strap that you fasten across your body when travelling in a vehicle _ _ _ _ _ _ _ _ _

h the fastest speed that a vehicle is allowed to travel on a particular road _ _ _ _ _ _ _ _ _ _

i fuel that does not contain lead
  _ _ _ _ _ _ _ _ _ _ _ _ _ _

E✗tra practice

Plan a 20-day trip to South Africa. Look at a guidebook or the Internet and find places that you would like to visit. Then look at a map and plan your route.

Can-do checklist

Tick what you can do.

	Can do	Need more practice
I can search a text for abbreviations and particular words.	✔	✔
I can find out what car rental payments include.		
I can understand driving laws and road safety advice.		

Unit 3
Somewhere to live

go to Useful language p. 83

Get ready to read

- Circle the words in these sentences so that they are true for you.
  I live *on my own / with other people*.
  I live in a *flat / house*.
  I *own / rent* the property.
  I *share a room / have my own room*.

- How would you try to find accommodation if you moved to a different town or country? Tick ✓ the things you would do.
  I'd go to an accommodation agency. ☐
  I'd look in the newspaper. ☐
  I'd advertise in the newspaper. ☐
  I'd look on the Internet. ☐
  I'd advertise on the Internet. ☐
  I'd ask friends if they knew of any accommodation. ☐

A Looking for a room

Learning tip

The texts in this book are real texts written for ordinary people. These people read the texts with a purpose in mind – for example, people read accommodation advertisements like those in this unit because they want a place to live.
When you read a text, ask yourself: Who would read this text? Why would they read it? Understanding who would read something, and why, will help you to read the text as if you were reading it in the real world.

1 Imagine you are moving to a new town and want to rent a room. What do you need to know about a room before you see it? Look at the examples, and then write four more questions.

When is it available?
Is it near the town centre?

----

2 Look at these internet advertisements for accommodation in and around Cambridge. Can you find the answers to all your questions in each advertisement?

File   Edit   View   Favorites   Tools   Help
Address [   ] [→] Go   Links »

a   Chesterton, double room for non-smoker in friendly mixed shared house, let from beginning February, £225 per calendar month excluding bills. Call 07967 920745.

b   Ground-floor single bedroom with own bathroom. Suit professional male. £85 per week including bills. Ten minutes from city centre on foot. Email: boxleyrooms@hotmail.co.uk

c   Available 8 January for eight months: two furnished rooms in fabulous new house near A14. All modern conveniences – double glazing, gas central heating, power shower, etc. Broadband, off-road parking. £455 per month all inclusive. References required. Phone 01223 34109 evenings.

d   Female wanted for a nice furnished room in a family home, £75 per week, all inclusive. Move in as soon as possible. Long or short term. Phone Carol 01223 73926.

3 Look at the newspaper advertisements on the right, which are also for accommodation in and around Cambridge. Why are they more difficult to understand than the internet advertisements?

4 Work out the meaning of the abbreviations in the newspaper advertisements. If you need some help, you will find all these words in the internet advertisements.

Advertisement e
sgl rm: ___single room___   nr: _____   f n/s: _____
pcm all incl: _____   avail beg Jan: _____

Advertisement f
mins: _____   d/g + gas c/h: _____   ASAP: _____
mths: _____   Refs req.: _____

Advertisement g
1 bed: _____   furn: _____   prof couple: _____
mod cons: _____   pcm excl bills: _____   eves: _____

Advertisement h
dbl rm: _____   m owner: _____   pw incl bills: _____

5 Look again at advertisements a–h. Find the best accommodation for each of these people. Read the example before you begin.

Ryuichi is from Japan. He works as a translator for a company in the centre of Cambridge. When Ryuichi came to Britain, he started smoking again. __b__

> The room in advertisement b is near the centre of town and is suitable for a professional male. Also, the advertisement doesn't ask for a non-smoker.

Julia is only in Cambridge for two months. She wants to live with a British family so that she can improve her English as much as possible. _____
Marina and **Stefan** have just got married. Marina has a job teaching German in a secondary school. They don't particularly want to share accommodation with other people. _____
Pei Lan is studying in Cambridge from the beginning of January until the end of June when she goes back home to Taiwan. Some of her friends are studying in London and she sometimes visits them there. _____
Ibrahim is from Qatar. He has a car, which he uses most weekends. His cousin is arriving in Cambridge very soon. He is going to study at the same language school as Ibrahim and also needs a room. _____
Mirella would like to share with women, preferably British ones. She doesn't smoke or drive and is happy to rent a small room. _____
Tolga works in a hotel outside Cambridge and he drives there every day. He now has a small room and would like something larger. _____
Aleksy doesn't want to pay more than £60 a week. He doesn't want to live on his own or with a family. He's a non-smoker. _____

6 Imagine you are going to study English in Cambridge and need somewhere to live. Would you be interested in any of the accommodation in advertisements a–h? Why? / Why not?

e
Lovely, sgl rm in shared house nr city centre, f n/s, £295 pcm all incl, avail beg Jan. Email: Jane6@virgin.net

f
Large room, 2 mins railway station, d/g + gas c/h, let from ASAP for 6 mths. Refs req. 07822 867544

g
Wood Road, 1 bed furn flat, suit prof couple, all mod cons. £500 pcm excl bills + deposit. Phone Gloria on 01223 43673 eves.

h
Sunny dbl rm, house shared with m owner, garage, £70 pw incl bills. Phone Steve on 01223 56220.

Did you know ...?

If you are looking for a room to rent in the UK, you will find advertisements in the local newspaper, in newsagents' and post office windows, and on the Internet. You may also be able to get a list of accommodation agencies from the local Tourist Information Office.

Class bonus

Work in pairs and write an advertisement for a room. Use abbreviations where possible. Exchange your advertisements with other pairs of students. Find a room you would like to rent.

E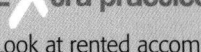tra practice

Look at rented accommodation in the UK at the website www.roomsforlet.co.uk Find a room you would like to rent.

B Signing a contract

Did you know …?

You usually have to sign a tenancy agreement before you move into a room, flat or house that you are going to rent. When you sign a tenancy agreement, you need a witness. This person watches you sign to confirm that your signature is genuine.

The language of these agreements can be old-fashioned and formal – even native English speakers have problems understanding it. However, a tenancy agreement is a legally binding contract so it is very important to understand what you are signing. If a tenant – the person who is renting the flat – breaks one of the conditions, the landlord – the owner – could take them to court.

1 On pages 18 and 19 you looked at some advertisements and matched them with people looking for accommodation. Scan this tenancy agreement and answer these questions.

a Which person from page 19 signed this agreement?

----

b Which property from page 18 or 19 is the agreement for?

----

c Who witnessed the tenant's signature?

----

d What do we know about the tenant's witness?

TENANCY AGREEMENT

DEFINITIONS

THE LANDLORD Mrs Gloria Black of 6 Sutton Road, Cambridge CB5 7AQ
THE TENANT Marina Kahn
PROPERTY 24a Wood Road, Cambridge CB2 8BG
TOGETHER WITH CONTENTS (fixtures, furniture and equipment) specified in the inventory (attached)
TERM from 1st January 20__ to 31st December 20__ (12 months)
RENT £500 per calendar month, payable in advance on the first day of each month
DEPOSIT £500, payable on commencement of this Agreement

AGREEMENTS

A The Landlord may re-enter the Property and terminate this Agreement if the Rent or any part of it is not paid within fourteen days after it becomes due.

B The Landlord may bring the tenancy to an end at any time before the expiry of the Term (but not earlier than six months from the Commencement Date of this Contract) by giving the Tenant not less than two months' written notice stating that the Landlord requires possession of the Property.

C The Landlord shall put the deposit with The Deposit Protection Service, and shall inform the Tenant within 14 days of taking the deposit of the contact details of this service and details of how to apply for the release of the deposit from this service.

TENANT'S OBLIGATIONS

1 Pay the Rent into the Landlord's bank account at the times specified; and pay interest of 15 per cent per annum on any rent which is more than 14 days overdue.

2 Pay for all water, gas and electricity consumed on the Property during the Term; and pay in full for all charges made for the use of the telephone on the Property during the Term; and pay in full any council tax liable on the Property.

3 Keep the interior of the Property during the Term in a good and clean state of repair, condition and decoration; and make good all damage and breakages to the Property and its contents which may occur during the Term.

4 Permit the Landlord to enter the Property at all reasonable times: to inspect the Property and its contents; and to carry out any works of maintenance or repair to the Property which the Landlord may consider to be necessary; to show prospective new Tenants around the Property at the end of the tenancy.

5 Not take in any paying guest without the prior written consent of the Landlord.

6 Not use the Property other than as a private dwelling; nor carry on any profession, trade or business in the Property.

7 Not use any musical instrument, wireless or television between midnight and 7 am, nor permit any singing or dancing between these hours.

8 Not fix a wireless or television aerial to the exterior of the Property; nor fix any notice, sign, advertisement or poster to the exterior or windows of the Property.

9 Not keep in the Property any cat, dog or other pet without the prior written consent of the Landlord.

10 Deliver up the Property to the Landlord at the end of the tenancy in the same good and clean state of repair, condition and decoration as it was in at the commencement of the Term (fair wear and tear, and damage by accidental fire excepted).

SIGNATURES

Tenant: Name (print): **MARINA KAHN**   Signed: *Marina Kahn*
Witnessed by: Name (print): ALICE RACE   Signed: A. Race
                     Occupation: Secondary school teacher
                     Address: 16 School House Lane, Cambridge, CB2 8GH

Landlord: Name (print): GLORIA BLACK   Signed: Gloria Black
Witnessed by: Name (print): OLIVE LYDIA LEE   Signed: Olive L Lee
                     Occupation: Librarian
                     Address: 3 Fieldhead Road, Peterborough PB4 8DU

2 Marina asks Alice to explain the agreement. Look at the *Definitions* and *Agreements* sections. Then circle the correct words in Alice's explanations.

a   The tenancy starts on 1 January and lasts for *six /* *twelve* months.

b   If you don't pay your March rent before *1 March /* *15 March*, Gloria can ask you to leave the property.

c   If Gloria needs the flat, she must write to you *two /* *three* months before she wants you to leave.

d   Gloria *will / won't* keep your deposit in her bank account.

e   She *must / needn't* tell you how to get your deposit back.

3 Look at the *Tenant's Obligations* section. Match Alice's explanations a–j with points 1–10.

a   You can't listen to music during the night. ......*point 7*......

b   You can't put anything on the outside wall of the flat.
....

c   You have to pay the rent on the first day every month.
....

d   You have to let Gloria into the flat if she wants to look at it. ....

e   When you leave the flat, the flat must be as clean as it is now. ....

f   You have to pay all your bills. ....

g   You must get Gloria's permission in writing if you want a friend to stay and pay part of the rent. ....

h   You can't set up a business in the flat. ....

i   You must get Gloria's permission in writing before you get a pet. ....

j   You have to look after the flat properly. ....

4 Answer Marina's questions with *yes* or *no*. Underline the information in the agreement which gives the answer.

a   Do we have to pay council tax?   ...*yes*...

b   If we pay the rent more than 14 days late, do we have to pay interest?

c   Can we have all-night parties?

d   Do we have to pay for the telephone?

e   Can Gloria show new tenants around the flat while we're still here?

f   Can we put notices in the windows?

Focus on ...
formal language

There are many formal words and phrases in this tenancy agreement. For example, *terminate*, means 'to end' and *becomes due* means 'is owed' in Agreement A.

Find these phrases in the tenancy agreement, and circle the correct informal equivalent of the word(s) in *italics*.

a   the *expiry* of the Term   beginning / end

b   the *Commencement* Date   beginning / end

c   written *notice*   advice / warning

d   *inform* the tenant   ask / tell

e   water, gas and electricity *consumed*   used / provided

f   prior written *consent*   agreement / arrangement

g   the *exterior* of the Property   top / outside

Can-do checklist

Tick what you can do.

	Can do	Need more practice
I can put myself in the position of someone reading advertisements in the real world.		
I can understand advertisements for rented accommodation.		
I can work out the meaning of abbreviations.		
I can understand a tenancy agreement.		

Unit 4
I'll check it in

go to Useful language p. 83

Get ready to **read**

○ Look at the luggage in the picture and circle the correct words.
  a rucksack / vanity case
  b garment bag / suitcase
  c briefcase / holdall
  d suitcase / vanity case
  e garment bag / holdall
  f briefcase / rucksack

○ Which of these items of luggage do you usually travel with?

A How much luggage have you got?

1 **Miklós is going to fly from Paris to Toronto on an Air Canada flight. He knows he can take one bag as hand luggage (or 'carry-on baggage'). However, he doesn't know how much luggage he can check in, so he looks on the Air Canada website. Skim this webpage. Is it the one he needs?**

Learning tip

We usually look at a text quickly to find out what it is about. This type of reading is called skimming. When we skim, we get the main idea and don't pay attention to the small details. Skimming is very often the first step in reading a text.

○○○

AIR CANADA ✹

Checked Baggage Allowances

Customers are allowed to check the following amounts of luggage free of charge:

	Maximum number of bags (per person)	Maximum weight per bag	Maximum linear dimensions per bag (length + height + width)
Economy Class	2 bags	23 kg (50 lb)	158 cm (62 in)
Executive Class, Executive First and Star Alliance Gold	3 bags	32 kg (70 lb) Total weight of all 3 bags not to exceed 69 kg (150 lb)	158 cm (62 in)
Air Canada Elite and **Super Elite** (in any class of service)	4 bags	32 kg (70 lb) Total weight of all 4 bags not to exceed 92 kg (200 lb)	158 cm (62 in)

lb = pound   kg = kilogram   in = inch   cm = centimetres

2 **Does the webpage give the information in a–d below? Skim the webpage again and tick ✓ one or more of the boxes.**
  a the size of the luggage passengers can check in ☐
  b the weight of the luggage passengers can check in ☐
  c the number of items of luggage passengers can check in ☐
  d the cost of checking in excess baggage ☐

3 **Miklós is planning to travel Economy Class. Find out the following.**
  a the largest size suitcase he can check in

  ----

  b the total weight of luggage he can check in

  ----

4 Miklós wants to check in more luggage than his free allowance, so he looks at the Excess Baggage Fees webpage. Skim the webpage and find three situations when you have to pay an excess baggage fee to Air Canada.

AIR CANADA 🍁

Excess Baggage Fees

When travelling on Air Canada, the size and number of bags you check is limited by the <u>free checked baggage allowance</u>. If your baggage exceeds this free allowance (too many pieces, too big or too heavy), you will be charged an excess baggage fee.

Excess baggage is accepted subject to space availability. Currency exchange may affect amount to be paid. Applicable taxes are not included in the prices.

Note: Please arrive at the airport at least 60 min before departure if checking overweight or oversized baggage. More than one excess fee may be applied. For example, if the item is overweight and oversize, it will be charged twice.

For oversized (more than 115 in / 292 cm) or overweight bags (more than 70 lb / 32 kg), please contact your <u>Air Canada Cargo Local Sales Office</u> for handling.

Economy Class

Type of excess	Restriction	Excess Fee More than one excess fee may be applied.
Overweight	Between 23 kg and 32 kg (50 lb–70 lb)	$35 CAD ($30 USD) per bag
Oversized*	Between 160 cm and 292 cm (63 in–115 in)	$35 CAD ($30 USD) per bag
Extra baggage More than 2 bags	North America (Canada/US/Mexico)	$105 CAD ($91 USD) per bag
	International (all other destinations) **	$175 CAD ($152 USD) per bag

* Sizes indicate linear dimensions per bag (length + width + depth)
** Excludes Brazil and Japan (Please contact Air Canada Reservations for details on excess fees to these destinations)

---

5 Miklós wants to check in this luggage. What excess baggage fee will he have to pay? Tick ✓ one of the boxes.

$35 CAD ☐ $70 CAD ☐ $105 CAD ☐

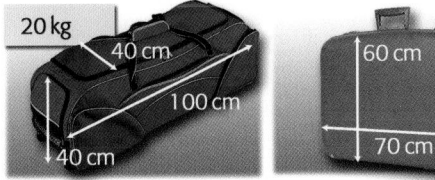

6 Other Economy Class passengers on Miklós's flight want to check in the following items of luggage. Will each passenger have to pay an excess baggage fee? Write *Y* (yes) or *N* (no).

a two medium-sized suitcases – one weighing 22 kg and the other weighing 30 kg ..Y..

b two large suitcases – each measuring more than 160 cm, but weighing less than 23 kg ......

c two medium-sized suitcases – all within the weight and size restrictions ......

d one suitcase weighing 22 kg, with the following dimensions: 80 x 40 x 30 cm ......

7 **Have you ever paid an excess baggage fee? How much did you have to pay?**

Focus on ...
the prefix *over*

A prefix is a group of letters which you add to the beginning of one word to make another.

Complete these sentences with *over* and the words from the list.

> crowded ~~done~~ due grown priced rated

a If vegetables are cooked too long, they are <u>overdone</u>.

b If a garden is full of plants that have become too big, it is ....

c If you forget to take your book back to the library, it is ....

d If there are too many people in a place, it is ....

e If a film is considered to be better than it really is, it is ....

f If something is too expensive, it is ....

Class bonus

Think of five items you cannot travel without. Compare your list with someone else's. Are any of your items the same?

B **Where's my luggage?**

1 Miklós flies from Paris Charles de Gaulle Airport to Lester B Pearson International Airport in Toronto. Unfortunately, when he goes to Baggage Reclaim his holdall and suitcase do not appear. What do you think he should do? Write your answer.

I think _____

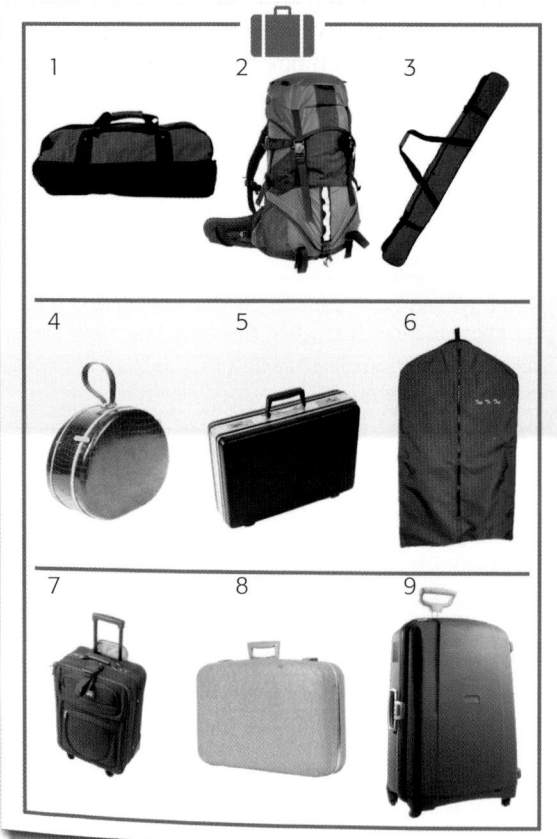

2 Miklós goes to the lost luggage desk to ask for help and is shown a card which illustrates different types of luggage. Look at the pictures on the card and match them with the descriptions below. Write the number in the boxes.

a medium hardshell suitcase [8]
b briefcase [ ]
c large rucksack [ ]
d ski bag [ ]
e small soft-sided trolley suitcase [ ]
f extra-large holdall [ ]
g large hardshell trolley suitcase [ ]
h garment bag [ ]
i vanity case [ ]

3 Miklós is given this form to fill in. Read the introduction. Should he be optimistic about getting his luggage back soon?

Missing items

Dear Customer

We are sorry that your baggage was mishandled during your recent flight and would be grateful if you could complete the form below to assist us in tracing it.

We would like to assure you that every effort will be made to locate your baggage and return it to you as soon as possible. We are pleased to report that the vast majority of delayed bags are found and returned to their owners within 48 hours.

If your baggage has not been located within 48 hours, we will continue to trace it for a maximum of three months.

PLEASE WRITE CLEARLY USING BLOCK CAPITALS

NAME: _____

ADDRESS AT DESTINATION: _____

TELEPHONE/MOBILE NUMBER: _____

DATE OF TRAVEL: _____

FROM: _____ TO: _____

FLIGHT NUMBER: _____ BAGGAGE CHECK NUMBER: _____

TYPE OF ITEM	SIZE	COLOUR

Signature _____ Date _____

4 Use the information from Miklós's boarding card, the label on his rucksack and his baggage check label to fill in the missing items form. Remember to include information about his checked baggage in the picture on the right.

Class | Classe
ECONOMY CLASS
name
MIKLÓS PILZINSKY
seat **33B**
Boarding time
Heure d'embarquement ▶
departure airport   To | Destination
PARIS CDG
date **26th NOV**
flight   time
AIR CANADA 854   13.30
Boarding Pass | Carte d'accès à bord

NAME Miklós Pilzinsky
DESTINATION ADDRESS 12-111
carlton Tower Road, Toronto,
Ontario M4C 5L6
TELEPHONE (001) 416 333 4276
DESTINATION AIRPORT Toronto,
Lester B Pearson International

AIR CANADA
PILZINSKY
CDG   26NOV   13.30
TO: TORONTO
AC 854
0014   AC790278

Did you know ...?

Charles de Gaulle (1890–1970) was a French general who was the first President of the Fifth Republic (1959–1969).

Lester Bowles Pearson (1897–1970) was a senior advisor to the UN, President of the UN General Assembly (1952–3) and Canadian Prime Minister. He won the Nobel Peace Prize in 1957.

E✗tra practice

What should Miklós do if he doesn't get his luggage back? Look at the website www.aircanada.com Does it have any information about delayed baggage?

Can-do checklist

Tick what you can do.

	Can do	Need more practice
I can skim a webpage to get a general idea of what it is about.	✓	✓
I can find out how much checked baggage I can take on a plane.		
I can fill in a form about delayed luggage.		

Unit 5
I'll be at home

Get ready to **read**

- Which of these items of mail do you often receive? Tick ✓ one or more of the boxes.
  personal letters ☐   postcards ☐   official letters ☐   bills ☐
  goods you ordered ☐   junk mail ☐   perishable goods like food, flowers ☐

- Think about postal services in your country and decide if the following sentences are true (T) or false (F) for you.
  My mail is delivered through the letterbox in my front door. _____
  I collect my mail from a PO Box at my local post office. _____
  I sometimes have to sign for letters or parcels. _____
  I sometime have to collect letters or parcels from the post office. _____
  If I want to send something very quickly, I have to pay extra for special delivery. _____

go to Useful language p. 83

A Sorry, you were out

1 It is one o'clock on Monday 23 March. Raquel Ramos García has just come home to find this card with her mail. Scan it and complete the sentences.

a The card is from _____

b The card is for _____

c The card has been put through Raquel's door because

_____

2 Look at the back of the card below. What would be a good heading for this side of the card? Tick ✓ one of the boxes.

a We'll call again ☐

b How to get your item ☐

c Royal Mail Services in your area ☐

Royal Mail

Sorry, you were out

| Time 12.32 | Today's date 23 March |

Name Raquel Ramos García
Address 133 Charlton Road
          Reading   Postcode RG24 7AW

You were out and your
☐ Special Delivery   ☐ Letter   ☐ International item
☑ Recorded Signed For ☐ Packet   ☐ Perishable item
could not be delivered to you   ☐ Large item

because
☑ A signature is required
☐ It's too big for your letterbox
Please see overleaf for information on where your item is now.

Item number ZH 5631 8734 5GB
Delivery person duty number

www.royalmail.com/redelivery

Your item has been left:
☐ In your 'Safeplace' on your property at:
☐ with your designated neighbour at:

☑ **Has been returned to the Royal Mail Delivery Office at:**
Royal Mail
Reading Delivery Office
84 Caversham Road
Reading,
Berkshire, RG1 1AA   TEL: 08456 113 227
HOURS: MON-FRI: 0600 - 1800
          SAT: 0600 - 1230

You can:
Collect the item. Please leave ☐2☐ hours before collecting. You'll need to bring evidence of your identity such as a passport or bank card. If someone's collecting on your behalf, they'll need to provide proof of your identity.

Redelivery or "Local Collect" services:
to arrange visit us online at **www.royalmail.com/redelivery** or call the number above.
We can **Redeliver** to your address or to an alternative local address (unfortunately, we can't redeliver Special Delivery items to an alternative address).
Or for 50p you can have your item taken to a local Post Office® Branch for you to pick up using our **"Local Collect"** service.

Please note we'll keep a Recorded item for 1 week, and all other items for 3 weeks before returning them to the sender.

Did you know ...?

Reading is a large town on the River Thames between London and Oxford. The pronunciation of Reading, the city, is /redɪŋ/. (What you are doing with this book is /riːdɪŋ/.) Note also that the pronunciation of the administrative region – or county – Berkshire is /baːkʃə/.

Learning tip

We often skim a text the first time we read it – we read it quickly to get a general sense. Alternatively, we scan a text – we read it quickly to find a particular piece of information. After a quick read, we sometimes go back and read parts of the text more carefully to find out further, more detailed information. We can use any combination of these different reading skills to find the information we need.

3 **Scan the front and back of the card on the opposite page and choose the correct ending for these sentences. Tick ✓ one of the boxes.**

a Raquel's item of mail is
   in the shed in the garden. ☐
   with a neighbour. ☐
   going back to the Delivery Office. ☐

b The earliest she can collect the item is
   2.00 pm. ☐
   2.32 pm. ☐
   two hours after finding the card. ☐

4 **Raquel asks a neighbour to explain how to get her item of mail. Read the back of the card again and decide if what the neighbour says is true (T) or false (F). Correct the information that is wrong.**

a If you go and collect the letter yourself, you have to prove that you're the person it's addressed to. _T_

b If someone else goes for you, they have to show their passport or bank card. _____

c You have to phone if you want to collect the letter. _____

d They charge extra if you have the letter delivered to someone else's house. _____

e You have to pay if you want to collect the letter from your nearest post office. _____

f You have four weeks from when you get the card to collect your letter. _____

5 **Raquel wants her mail to be redelivered to a friend's house on Wednesday. She goes to www.royalmail.com/redelivery to arrange this. Read the webpage below and decide which friend Raquel's mail should be redelivered to.**

a Claudia Santos, 3 Harris Gardens, Reading RG17 3PE ☐

b Sam Williams, 15 St Mary's Way, Reading RG24 6TR ☐

c Aisha Hussein, Flat 2, 26 Water Lane, Reading RG12 1RR ☐

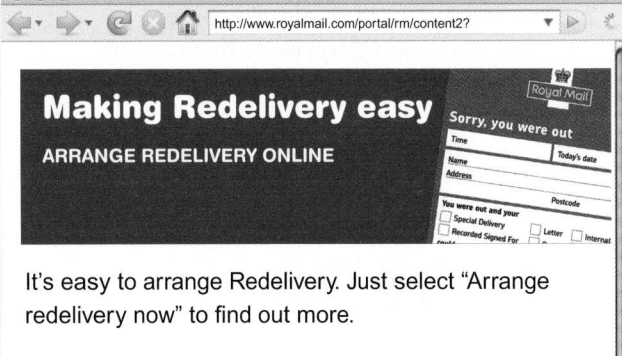

It's easy to arrange Redelivery. Just select "Arrange redelivery now" to find out more.

Redeliver to your own address

We can redeliver your item to your address on a day that is convenient to you, free of charge.

Redeliver to a different address

With the exception of Special Delivery services, we can deliver your item to a different address within the same postcode area, e.g. a neighbour's house, free of charge. A postcode area is determined by your local Delivery Office, and is the area that they deliver to. We cannot redeliver to an address outside of this area. In most cases, for example, if you live in SE25 the same postcode area would be any other postcode starting with SE25.

Class bonus

Raquel decides to have the item delivered to her friend's house on Wednesday. Why does she choose this option, do you think? Why doesn't she choose any of the other options? How many reasons can you suggest?

Work with a partner and discuss your answers. Have you got any different reasons?

B Run the cold tap

1 Raquel also finds a leaflet with her mail. Scan the back of the leaflet on the right and find the answers to these questions.

a Who is the leaflet from?

----

b Who is it for?

----

c Why has it been put through the door?

----

2 Skim the inside of the leaflet below. Which of these things does this part of the leaflet do? Tick ✓ one or more of the boxes.

a explains in general terms why the water has to be turned off ☐

b explains exactly why the water has to be turned off on Saturday ☐

c gives advice about what to do while the water is turned off ☐

d gives advice about what to do when the water is turned on again ☐

Thames Water

interruptions
to your **water** supply

Warning of essential work in your area

This is notice of essential work in your area that will interrupt your water supply

We will have to turn off your water supply for

............2............ hours on ..28 March..

If the water is turned off for more than 6 hours, you can get water from

----

The table below shows when the interruptions to your water supply are likely to start

	Morning	Afternoon
Monday		
Tuesday		
Wednesday		
Thursday		
Friday		
Saturday	X	
Sunday		

Why we need to interrupt your water supply

We supply drinking water to over seven million customers through nearly 31,000 km of pipes. We are spending £1 million a day to ensure this service is provided, because these pipes sometimes need attention. In order to do this, we have to cut off your water supply from time to time because of planned or urgent work.

For your guidance

Do not use any household appliances that would normally use water, including a washing machine or dishwasher, while the water is off.

Switch your central heating system off.

Once the water supply returns

Please run the cold tap nearest to the inlet pipe, which is normally in the kitchen.

Allow at least 2–5 minutes until the water runs clear.

If your water does not come back on then please:

• Check with a neighbour to see if their supply has been restored

• Check that the inside stop valve* is fully open by turning it off and turning it on again

If this does not solve the problem

Please call us on **0845 9200 800** (all calls are charged at local rates)

Thank you for your co-operation.

*A valve is a device which opens and closes to control the flow of liquids or gases.

3 Raquel is going to be at home on Saturday, 28 March. Which of these things can she do that morning? Circle *can* or *can't* so that the sentences are correct.

a She can / can't use the vacuum cleaner.
b She *can* / *can't* do her washing.
c She *can* / *can't* have the central heating on.
d She *can* / *can't* flush the toilet.
e She *can* / *can't* use the microwave.

4 It is now Sunday. This is what happened on Saturday afternoon. Read the inside of the leaflet again to help you put the events in the correct order.

a The Thames Water representative told her the water would be reconnected by five o'clock. ☐
b She tried the tap again at two o'clock in the afternoon, and there was still no water. ☑2
c The neighbour said that her water had come back on at half past twelve. ☐
d Raquel tried the tap at midday Saturday, but there was no water. ☑1
e She turned on the cold tap in the kitchen and let it run for five minutes. ☐
f She asked her neighbour if her water had come back on. ☐
g She called 0845 9200 800 because she still didn't have any water. ☐
h Two hours later Raquel was in the bathroom when she discovered that the water was back on. ☐
i Raquel checked the stop valve and it seemed to be fully open. ☐
j Then she had her shower. ☐

Focus on ...
phrasal verbs

Complete these extracts from the inside of the leaflet with three phrasal verbs which include the word *off*. Do all three phrasal verbs have the same meaning?
a … we have to ......*cut*...... off your water supply
b .... your central heating system off.
c Check that the inside stop valve is fully open by .... it off

The position of the object varies with phrasal verbs, depending on whether the object is a noun or a pronoun. If it is a noun, it can come before or after the particle (e.g. *pick the letter up* / *pick up the letter*). If the object is a pronoun, it can only come before the particle (*pick it up*).

Which of these rewordings of a–c are also correct? Tick ✓ the boxes.
d we have to cut your water supply off ☐
e we have to cut it off ☐
f we have to cut off it ☐
g Switch off your central heating system. ☐
h Switch off it. ☐
i Switch it off. ☐
j Check that the inside stop valve is fully open by turning off the valve ☐
k Check that the inside stop valve is fully open by turning the valve off ☐
l Check that the inside stop valve is fully open by turning off it ☐

E✗tra practice

Look at the website: www.thameswater.co.uk Use the quick links to find how to save water at home. Are there any tips that you can use?

Can-do checklist

Tick what you can do.

	Can do	Need more practice
I can use a variety of skills when reading texts.	✓	✓
I can follow instructions about having my mail redelivered.		
I can follow instructions about having my water supply interrupted.		

Unit 6
A weekend in Wales

Get ready to read

- Label the countries of the United Kingdom with the names in the box.

  | England   Northern Ireland   Scotland   Wales |

- How much do you know about Wales? Which of these sentences do you think are true? Tick ✓ one or more of the boxes.
  a The national sport of Wales is golf. ☐
  b Some people speak Welsh as their first language. ☐
  c Wales is a wonderful holiday destination for people who like walking, climbing and other outdoor pursuits. ☐
  d Wales has three national parks which include beautiful mountains and coastal areas. ☐

a _____

d _____

c _____   b _____

go to Useful language p. 83

A Find your Welsh holiday here

1 **Sebastian is asking his friend Geraint about places to visit in Wales. Look at what Geraint says. Is he recommending St David's, or is he advising Sebastian not to go there?**

Learning tip

Think about what you already know about a topic before you read a text about it. This allows you to relate what you read to what you already know, and it makes the new text easier to understand.

> St David's is like a village, but it's called a city because it's got a cathedral.

> The coast's beautiful around there – and if you get good weather, it's wonderful walking along the Coast Path.

> We went to an island where there were loads of birds – and no people.

> You can go surfing near St David's – the beaches and waves are wonderful, but the water's freezing!

2 **Sebastian decides to visit St David's, so he looks for some accommodation on the Internet. He finds the webpage opposite about a bed and breakfast. What extra information is there on it about the things Geraint mentioned? Read the webpage and complete the sentences.**

a St David's is _the smallest city in Europe._
b On the Coast Path _____
c The beaches _____
d There are birds _____

Did you know ...?

The population of Wales is about three million (5% of the UK population) and its capital is Cardiff. With its mountainous landscape and numerous sandy beaches, Wales has always attracted a lot of tourists. In 2002, for example, nearly 13 million trips of one night or more were made in Wales, generating expenditure of £1.8 billion. 11.9 million of these trips were made by UK residents.

File   Edit   View   Favorites   Tools   Help

Address http://www.stayinwales.co.uk/detail.cfm?i=1989   Go   Links »

StayinWales.co.uk
find your Welsh holiday here

Bed & Breakfast – St David's

Ramsey House

Catering exclusively for adults, Ramsey House offers you professional hotel standards of accommodation and food service coupled with the friendly, relaxed atmosphere of a high-class non-smoking guest house.

Situated within walking distance of St David's, the smallest city in Europe, the house stands in its own attractive gardens and has private off-road parking. In the opposite direction, there is easy access to the Pembrokeshire Coast Path, where you can see some of Britain's most spectacular coastal scenery with its abundant bird life and wild flowers.

We have three double and three twin rooms. Each is individually furnished and decorated to 4-star standard with comfortable beds, central heating, remote control colour TV, hospitality trays, hair dryers and plenty of mirrors. All the rooms have a modern, well-lit en-suite bathroom with WC, shaver socket and electric shower.

All first-floor rooms have views of either the sea, the Cathedral or open country, and there are three ground-floor rooms with garden views, ideal for guests unable to climb stairs.

Our full Welsh breakfast offers you a great start to the day with homemade bread, muffins, marmalade and preserves. We can also prepare fresh picnic lunches for your day out walking the Coast Path or on the beaches.

There is a comfortable lounge with lots of books and leaflets about Pembrokeshire to help you plan your excursions. Weather permitting, guests may enjoy the peace and tranquillity of our gardens and watch the birds feeding. Drinks are served in both the garden and lounge.

We also have secure bicycle storage, a drying room and light laundry facilities.

Nearby are some of the safest and cleanest beaches in Europe offering a variety of water sports including sailing, surfing, wind-surfing and sea angling. Visitors are welcome at St David's City Golf Club and several other Pembrokeshire clubs. We are also conveniently situated for easy access to the bird sanctuary islands of Ramsey, Skomer and Skokholm.

A warm welcome awaits you at Ramsey House all year round. You will find it the ideal touring centre in all seasons.

Proprietors: Ceri & Elaine Morgan
01437 72021

3 Three of Sebastian's friends want to come to Wales with him. He writes an email to them about the accommodation. Complete his email.

From: Sebastian
Subject: B&B in Wales

Hi everyone,
I've found a ᵃ_bed and breakfast_ on the Internet. It's called ᵇ_____ , and it's in a great location between ᶜ_____ and the Pembrokeshire Coast Path. If we want to do some walking, it sounds a good place to stay because they provide ᵈ_____ (should save on lunch bills). Also, there's a ᵉ_____ which will be useful if we get soaking wet walking in the rain. Oh, and the rooms are all ᶠ_____ , so we won't all have to share one bathroom! (Pete, you won't have to miss *Match of the Day* because there's a TV in ᵍ_____ .) We can also take our bikes as there's ʰ_____ .
What do you think?
Seb

4 Read these profiles of different tourists. Do you think they would like to stay at Ramsey House? Write **Y** (yes) or **N** (no) and underline the parts of the webpage which help you decide.

a Ana is a wheelchair user who enjoys holidays by the coast. __Y__ ('ideal for guests unable to climb stairs')

b Daniel wants to stay in St David's. _____

c Sofia and Takis have just bought an expensive car and need safe parking. _____

d Tina and Xavier are a married couple with two young children. _____

5 If you were going to Wales, would you like to stay at Ramsey House? Why? / Why not?

E╳tra practice

Choose one of the places in the webpage (for example, St David's, the Pembrokeshire Coast Path, Skomer) and find out five more facts about it on the Internet or from books.

B Your room will be ready for you

1 Sebastian makes some notes about the accommodation he and his friends want. He then phones Ramsey House. Read his notes and write the questions he asks in his phone conversation.

a Have you got any rooms for four nights from 29 May? ....
b ....
c ....
d ....
e ....
f ....

tel: 01437 72021 MORGAN
4 nights: 29 May – 1 June incl?
4 people: 2 twin rooms?
Price?
Rooms available – what time?
Credit card?
Time we have to leave?

2 Sebastian received this letter on 20 May. Who is it from?

....

3 Read the letter and find out if Sebastian can have the accommodation he wants. Write an answer for each of your questions in Exercise 1.

a No, there are only rooms for three nights. ....
b ....
   ....
c ....
   ....
d ....
   ....
e ....
   ....
f ....
   ....

4 Answer these questions about the cost of the accommodation.

a How much has Sebastian already paid for the accommodation?
   £140
b How did he pay this?
   ....
c How much more will Sebastian and his friends have to pay at the end of their stay?
   ....
d How can they pay this?
   ....

Ramsey House

Lower Moor
St David's
Haverfordwest
Pembrokeshire SA62 6RP

Telephone: 01437 72021

Licensed Guest House

18 May 20__

Mr Sebastian Rose
Flat 1
7 Cartwright Street
Edinburgh
EH18 8E2

Dear Mr Rose

Thank you for your deposit cheque for £140. We have pleasure in reserving the following accommodation for you:

ROOM/S: **2 twin en-suite rooms**
DATES: **Saturday, 29 May – Monday, 31 May (3 nights)**
DEPARTING AFTER BREAKFAST: **Tuesday, June 1st**

Our tariff is £35 per person per night for bed and breakfast.

Please note we do not operate a credit card facility. You are welcome to settle your account by cheque or cash.

When you book your holiday you are entering into a legally binding contract. Should you cancel this reservation for any reason within 4 weeks of arrival, and we are unable to re-let the accommodation, you will be liable for a cancellation charge up to the total cost of your holiday. You may, therefore, wish to insure your holiday against cancellation when arranging your general travel insurance. No allowance is made for meals not taken.

Your room will be ready for you from 2.00 pm on your day of arrival when we will do all we can to ensure the enjoyment of your visit.

Yours sincerely,

Ceri Morgan

Ceri and Elaine Morgan

5 Which of these things does Ceri Morgan do in his letter? Tick ✓ one or more of the boxes and <u>underline</u> the parts of the letter where Ceri does these things.

a He thanks Sebastian for his phone call. ☐
b He cancels the reservation made over the phone. ☐
c He confirms Sebastian's reservation. ☐
d He explains the rules about cancelled reservations. ☐
e He advises Sebastian to arrange cancellation insurance. ☐
f He gives directions to Ramsey House. ☐

6 Unfortunately, Sebastian's friends are ill the week after he receives the letter, so he decides to cancel the holiday. He reads the letter again before he phones Ramsey House. Answer these questions.

a What might happen to the money Sebastian has already paid?
----
b Might Sebastian and his friends have to pay the rest of their bill?
----
c In what circumstances would they get their money back?
----
d Would it make a difference if Sebastian had holiday insurance?
----

7 Do you think the Morgans will manage to re-let the rooms Sebastian booked? Why? / Why not?

Focus on ...
should

In his letter, Ceri Morgan writes 'Should you cancel this reservation … you will be liable for a cancellation charge'. We sometimes use *should* instead of *if* in formal written English.

Complete these sentences with *should* and a verb from the list.

be change ~~damage~~ leave require ring see worsen

a ___Should___ you ___damage___ anything, you will be charged for it.
b _____ you _____ anyone in danger, you should call the coastguard.
c _____ we _____ out, you can collect the keys from next door.
d _____ you _____ anything behind, we will send it to you.
e _____ you _____ your mind, please return the goods within ten days.
f _____ the telephone _____ , please ignore it.
g _____ you _____ refreshments, we will be happy to provide tea and coffee.
h _____ the weather _____ , the trip will be cancelled.

Class bonus

Work in pairs. One person is Sebastian and the other is Ceri Morgan. Act out the conversation between them when Sebastian phones to cancel his reservation.
Sebastian: Explain why you have to cancel.
Ceri: Explain the cancellation rules.

Can-do checklist

Tick what you can do.

	Can do	Need more practice
I can relate information I already know to what I read in a text.		
I can understand a description of bed and breakfast accommodation.		
I can understand a letter of confirmation and the rules about cancelled accommodation.		

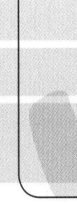

Unit 7
I saw an article about it

go to Useful language p. 84

Get ready to read

- Do you ever read magazines? Tick ✓ the magazines you read.
  business and/or current affairs magazines ☐   computer magazines ☐
  sports magazines ☐   magazines about celebrities ☐
  cookery magazines ☐   fashion and/or photography magazines ☐
  holiday and/or travel magazines ☐   car and/or bike magazines ☐

- When do you usually buy magazines? How many do you buy a month? Do you keep them?

A Call of the wild

1 Look at the article on the opposite page. What kind of magazine is it from?

_____

2 What can you see in the photograph? What kind of animal is it?

_____

Did you know ...?

The word *safari* comes from Swahili and Arabic. The Arabic word is *safar* meaning 'travel' or 'journey'. Swahili is one of the major languages of Kenya, Tanzania and Uganda.

Lots of words which are used in English have come from other languages. For example: *typhoon* (Chinese), *robot* (Czech), *cruise* (Dutch), *opera* (Italian), *judo* (Japanese), *ski* (Norwegian), *sofa* (Persian), *buffalo* (Portuguese), *yoghurt* (Turkish).

3 Match these headings with the paragraphs in the article. Write each paragraph number in the correct box.

- a Lodge or camp? ☐
- b Where to go? ☐
- c Drive, walk or boat? ☐
- d What about other activities? ☐
- e When to go? ☐ 1

4 Read paragraph 1. Do these sentences describe the dry season (D) or the wet season (W)?

- a There are more animals at each waterhole. D
- b There are more leaves on the trees and bushes. _____
- c You can't drive along some tracks. _____
- d There are fewer places to stay. _____
- e The animals can be seen more clearly. _____
- f Baby animals are born during this season. _____

5 Paragraphs 2 and 3 contrast several things. Read the paragraphs and think about the advantages of each situation below. Complete the sentences in your own words.

- a If you camp, _you are always in the bush and you are very close to the animals._
- b If you stay in a lodge, _____
  _____
- c If you go on a game drive, _____
  _____
- d If you go on a walking safari, _____
  _____
- e If you go on a boat, _____
  _____

6 Paragraphs 4 and 5 give several examples of travel destinations. Which region or country would you go to if you wanted to do these things?

- a see wildlife _East Africa, Namibia_
- b see beautiful scenery _____
- c do exciting activities _____
- d go on a relaxing boat trip _____
- e climb a mountain _____

Call of the wild

Old Africa hand Sandy Beatty gives five insider tips for choosing your first safari

[1] The dry season offers better game-viewing, as higher concentrations of animals congregate around fewer waterholes, with less foliage to hide behind. During the rains, some tracks become impassable and many camps close. However, in the wet season, animals – and consequently safari vehicles – are often more dispersed. Trees and shrubs are greener and in flower, and many newborn animals can be spotted. Weather's not the only consideration – visiting Kenya or Tanzania during the Great Migration (July–September), when more than one million wildebeest thunder across the Serengeti, is an experience of a lifetime.

[2] There's nothing quite like a top-end safari lodge for the classic Africa experience – crisp white tablecloths, cold drinks, impeccable service and usually a waterhole, or savannah viewpoint not too far away. But camping safaris get you right in among the action. Either way, with Explore* you will have a top-notch leader and you'll be spotting the same game – there's no such thing as a luxury lion.

[3] A 4WD game drive enables you to sample several different areas in a relatively short space of time. But walking safaris get you away from trails to enjoy the smaller creatures and quieter sounds of the bush. Boat safaris get you close to animals drinking from waterholes and rivers, and offer a unique perspective. For the ideal mix, why not combine more than one mode of transport?

[4] If you have a burning ambition to spot one particular species, check where to head for the best chance. For apes and the Great Migration, it has to be East Africa; for desert-adapted elephants or a close-up cheetah encounter, Namibia's the place. Trip dossiers will give you an idea of which species you can expect to see.

[5] Africa offers a lot more than just safaris. Head for Tanzania to tack on a Zanzibar beach break or to climb Kilimanjaro; to Zambia for Victoria Falls and some adrenalin action; to Kenya for Arab culture and dhow cruises; or to South Africa for fantastic landscapes, food and wine.

*Explore is a travel company.

7 Look at the headings in Exercise 3. Imagine you are going on safari. What are your own answers to the five questions in the headings?

Class bonus

Work with a partner. Ask and answer questions about your safari. For example, *When are you going to go? Are you going to camp?* Find out if you have chosen the same type of safari holiday as your partner. Work with several other students and find the person whose holiday plans are most similar to your own.

Focus on ...
vocabulary

There are some useful words about safari holidays in the article. Read these definitions of some of the words and write each word.

a wild animals (that are hunted or photographed) g a m e

b a small house in the country that is used especially by people on a sporting holiday _ _ _ _ _

c a path through the countryside _ _ _ _ _

d wild parts of Africa where very few people live

_ _ _ _ _ _ _ _ _

e a group of animals which share the same characteristics

_ _ _ _ _ _ _ _

f an animal like a large monkey _ _ _

B A walk in the park

1 You are going to read part of a magazine article which has the title 'A walk in the park'. Choose the correct adjective from the box to complete the sentence and find the meaning of the expression.

boring	cheap	difficult
easy	frightening	tiring

'A walk in the park' is something that is .... to do.

2 Look quickly at the introduction to the article. Which park is the walk in?

....

Learning tip

Journalists often begin factual magazine articles with dramatic true stories to catch the reader's attention. They give the factual information later. To tell these true stories, journalists might use direct speech, past tenses and personal pronouns (*I, he, we,* etc.). Look out for these things in an article and then you will be able to recognize which parts of it are the dramatic beginning and which parts give the factual information.

3 Read the first seven paragraphs of the article. How does the journalist, Narina, begin her article? Tick ✓ one of the boxes.

a She describes the Olifants Trail. ☐

b She describes why she chose the trail. ☐

c She describes what happened one day. ☐

A walk in the park

Kruger National Park is a very different place when explored on foot. **Narina Exleby** pulled on her walking shoes and joined the three-nights Olifants Trail to get up close to rhino, otters, skulls and crickets.

1 "That's your bush. If it charges, you get behind it," Nicol Coetsee whispered softly. Eight pairs of eyes widened behind him. The white rhino munched on sweet grass. Everyone stood still.

2 It's one thing for a rhino to pass three metres from your vehicle, but when you're watching it graze just 15 metres away from you, and you have only a flimsy piece of vegetation for cover, the feeling is quite different. When it turns and charges, and you have a 2,600 kilogram white rhino bull sprinting straight at you, it's blood chilling.

3 The ground shook and thundered and dust billowed up behind the rhino. As the distance between it and the vegetation grew shorter and shorter, everyone held their breath and stood dead still; you could have heard a butterfly land on a twig.

4 When Nicol and Tsambok – both trail rangers – shouted and waved their arms, the rhino realised we were humans, took fright and sprinted off in another direction. Once the dust had settled, Nicol explained it had been a case of mistaken identity – we weren't really the rhino's target. Someone in the group had coughed and, probably thinking it was another male in its territory, the rhino had hurtled over to enforce its territorial rights.

5 It's the kind of encounter people dream of – and dread – when they do a wilderness trail.

6 Wilderness trails in Kruger National Park offer three nights of bush solitude. There are seven wilderness areas, set aside for walking trails. These sections have been virtually untouched by humans. Each has a camp, which is basic but comfortable, and minimal roads – used only by a

7 few trail staff.

Olifants Trail Camp is situated on the banks of the Olifants River. In the pre-dawn mornings you'll wake up to the snorts of hippos. During the day, the call of a fish eagle pierces the midday heat and at night the moans and roars of lions drift into the camp.

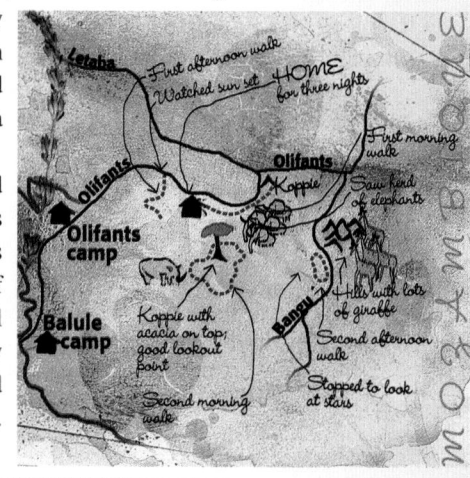

4 In which paragraph does Narina finish the dramatic beginning of her article?

----

5 What are the remaining paragraphs about?

----

6 Look at the map and find the rhino. When did Narina see it? Tick ✓ one of the boxes.

a On the first morning. ☐
b On the first afternoon. ☐
c On the second morning. ☐
d On the second afternoon. ☐

7 What happened when the group saw the rhino? Put these events in the correct order.

a Someone in the group coughed and the rhino heard this. ☐
b They saw a rhino 15 metres away. ☐1
c The rhino ran off in another direction. ☐
d Nicol told them what to do if the rhino charged. ☐
e Nicol and Tsambok shouted and waved their arms. ☐
f The rhino turned and ran towards the group. ☐

8 Why might people 'dream of – and dread' the situation Narina has just described? How would you have felt?

9 What would the rangers have done if the rhino had not run away? Have they ever had to do this? Read two later paragraphs from the article and find out.

Whenever we walked, the two trail rangers carried .458 calibre rifles. The group moved in single file with Nicol and Tsambok in front. "If we got into a dangerous situation, this would be the best position to be in," Nicol explained. "If Tsambok or I were at the back of the group, we would have to fire past eight people. Because we walk into the wind, the animals behind us or to our left or right are aware of our presence. It's the ones in front of us we have to worry about – the ones that we might stumble across and frighten."

Campfire talk

Around the dying campfire late one night, someone asked Nicol if he'd ever had any "funny incidents" with a group – a probing question that led to "so, have you ever had to use your gun?" One he must get asked often.

Nicol's eyes darkened. "Twice – incidents with elephants." His words were sketchy and his hands fidgeted. This was no fireside tale of bravado; this was the way life had to be in the bush. "I wouldn't have shot if I had been on my own." And he quietly left it at that.

10 Would you like to go on the Olifants Trail? Why? / Why not?

Can-do checklist

Tick what you can do.

	Can do	Need more practice
I can identify the main point in a paragraph.		
I can identify a dramatic beginning to an article.		
I can follow the order of events in a narrative.		

Unit 8
In the newspapers

go to Useful language p. 84

Get ready to read

- How often do you read a newspaper? _____

- Which of these sections of the newspaper do you read? Which do you read first? Why?
  TECHNOLOGY   CULTURE AND REVIEW   SPORT   NEWS
  FINANCIAL AND BUSINESS   HEALTH AND MEDICAL   TRAVEL

- Which sports are covered in the Sport section of the newspaper you read?
  _____

A Bikes are everywhere!

1 You are going to read the first part of three articles about cycling. Before you read, think about the newspaper sections in *Get ready to read*. What could a cycling article in each of the sections be about?

> An article in the Technology section could be about the latest developments in bike design.

2 Skim each extract on the opposite page and match it with one of the newspaper sections in *Get ready to read*.

Extract 1 _____
Extract 2 _____
Extract 3 _____

3 Read each extract and (circle) the words so that the sentences are true.

a 'Cooke shows ingredients for big prize' because *she is very fit / she has had a very successful season*.

b 'Cyclists facing £2,500 bell fines' could apply to *anyone who cycles / people who frequently cycle* without a bell.

c Andrew Ritchie has spent *a long time / a short time* developing 'The bicycle that turned into folding money'.

Did you know ...?

British and American daily newspapers, such as *The Independent* and *The Washington Post*, usually have a related Sunday equivalent – *The Independent on Sunday* and *The Washington Post Sunday Edition*. Sunday newspapers contain more sections and pages than daily newspapers. The 14 September 1987 edition of *The Sunday New York Times* weighed more than 5.4 kg and contained 1,612 pages.

Learning tip

Newspapers contain an enormous number and variety of reading texts, but most people do not read a newspaper from cover to cover. What we read depends on what we are interested in. We look at headlines, which summarize articles, and either read the article – part of it or all of it, again depending on our interest – or move on to another article. We read selectively.

4 Which is the most difficult extract for you to read? Think about the following:

- unknown words
- long words
- long sentences
- unfamiliar grammatical structures
- background information needed
- complicated order of information

5 Choose one of the extracts and read it carefully. List the main points.

_____
_____
_____

1

CYCLING WORLD CHAMPIONSHIPS

Cooke shows ingredients for big prize

by Jeremy Whittle

Is there any race that Nicole Cooke, the wonderfully talented cyclist from Wales cannot win? The 23-year-old will discover the answer to that question in Austria this week when she aims for an elusive World Championship crown.

Cooke will lead Team GB in Salzburg this week, at the climax of a phenomenal season during which she has emphasised her standing as the leading cyclist of her generation.

This year Cooke has risen to the top of the world rankings (the first British cyclist to do so), won the women's Tour de France, the World Cup series, the British National Championship, the Tour of New Zealand and several other significant events.

Apart from when she has had knee injuries, it has always been this way for Cooke. In 2001, she won world titles in road racing, time trialling and mountain biking. However, that triple crown came as a junior and a women's world title continues to elude her.

Full cycle: Cooke is favourite for success in Salzburg this week

2

Cyclists facing £2,500 bell fines

Tim Shipman

Cyclists could face fines of up to £2,500 for riding without a bell. New laws being considered by the Government would mean that every bike in Britain would have to be fitted with a bell.

Cycling without one would be a criminal offence, the same as dangerous riding, ignoring red lights or cycling on the pavement.

These offences typically attract fines of between £30 and £60.

But persistent offenders can be fined up to £2,500, have their driving licence endorsed or, in extreme cases, be jailed for 2 years.

Under current regulations, every bicycle has to be sold with a bell fitted. But there is no obligation for the rider to keep the bell after purchase.

Transport Minister Stephen Ladyman has now said it would be 'sensible' to extend cycling penalties to ensure that bells are not removed.

Sound advice: New bikes are fitted with bells, but there is nothing in law to stop cyclists removing them

3

The bicycle that turned into folding money

Ben Laurance meets Andrew Ritchie, an obsessive who has steered a portable bike into a British manufacturing success story

Meet Andrew Ritchie for the first time, and take in what you see: a lean, middle-aged man, slightly dishevelled, with one leg of his brown corduroy trousers tucked into his sock.

You might guess that he is a slightly posh gardener who has just cycled back from his latest landscaping project: he has something of the outdoor air about him. The tucked-in trouser leg gives him away as a cyclist.

And you would not be completely wrong. Yes, Andrew Ritchie used to be a landscape gardener. And yes, he's certainly a cyclist: each day, he pedals the six-and-a-bit miles from his home in South Kensington, west London to work on an unprepossessing industrial estate near Junction 2 of the M4.

But Ritchie, 58, is more than just another cyclist. He is a self-confessed obsessive, someone who has devoted the past 30 years of his life to building the best portable bicycle in the world, a machine that is fun and efficient to ride but can be quickly folded into a package smaller than an average suitcase, carried up and down stairs, tucked behind a train seat or secreted under a desk.

And it is an obsession that has reaped rewards. Ritchie controls and runs Brompton Bicycle, one of only two volume manufacturers still making bikes in Britain. No, it will never be on the scale of Raleigh, which in its heyday was producing a million frames a year and whose bikes are now imported. But since its inception, Brompton has made almost 100,000 of its distinctive 'folders'. It aims to produce nearly 14,000 in the coming year. It is a rarity – a British manufacturing success story.

---

6 Would you be interested in reading the rest of any of these articles? Why? / Why not? Would you rather choose an article of your own? What would that article be about?

Class bonus

Read the other extracts. Lightly underline any words or phrases that you don't understand. Work with a partner. Ask your friend if he/she knows the meaning of the text you have underlined. Help each other to understand the articles.

B Should I wear a helmet?

1 Label the picture with the words in the box.

cycle panniers   cycle path   fluorescent jacket   ~~helmet~~   lights

2 How can we make cycling safer? Tick ✓ one or more of the boxes.

Every cyclist should …
a … have a bell on their bike. ☐
b … cycle on the pavement. ☐
c … wear a helmet. ☐
d … ride on a cycle path. ☐
e … ignore traffic lights. ☐
f … have lights on their bike. ☐
g … wear fluorescent clothing. ☐
h … carry things in proper cycle panniers. ☐

a .... helmet ....

e ....

b ....

d ....

c ....

3 Look at the headline of the newspaper article below. Does this headline surprise you? Why? / Why not?

Cyclists with helmets 'more likely to be hit'

By **Ray Massey**
Transport Editor

Cyclists who wear helmets are more likely to be hit by overtaking vehicles, psychologists said last night.

Research reveals motorists drive more than three inches* closer to cyclists in helmets because they see them as more experienced.

However, female cyclists are given more room on the road than male cyclists, according to the survey.

The findings are being published by traffic psychologist Dr Ian Walker from the University of Bath. He used a bicycle fitted with an ultrasonic distance sensor to record data from more than 2,500 overtaking motorists.

After carrying out tests in Salisbury and Bristol, he said drivers were twice as likely to get closer to his bike when he had a helmet on.

Dr Walker said: 'This was something I had suspected, as many cyclists had told me of similar experiences.

'The perception is that those wearing helmets are more experienced and more predictable.

'Drivers think, "He knows what he's doing, he won't do anything surprising". But that's really quite a dangerous thought, particularly as so many cycling novices are told to wear helmets.'

Dr Walker was struck twice during the experiment.

Rider risk: Vehicles drive closer

Buses and trucks were the worst offenders. While the average car gave cyclists 52 inches of room, trucks got 7.5 inches closer and buses 9 inches.

Dr Walker wore a long wig to see if there was any difference in passing distance when vehicles thought they were overtaking a female cyclist. Vehicles gave him an average 6 inches more space.

He said this may be because women are seen as less predictable road users or because female cyclists are more rare and therefore treated with more caution.

Dr Walker wants his research to raise awareness of the dangers facing cyclists on busy roads.

Although road fatalities generally have fallen to a record low, cyclist deaths rose by an alarming ten per cent last year, official casualty figures revealed in June.

The number of riders killed in Britain increased to 148 in 2005 – the highest level since 1999.

The number seriously injured rose by two per cent to 2,212. Total casualties among cyclists, including those slightly injured, fell by one per cent in 2005 to 16,561.

Experts blame the rise in cycling deaths on the boom in the inexperienced 'green' riders taking to the road to beat congestion, reduce pollution and get fit.

Overtaking cars are thought to be the most dangerous hazard for riders. Dr Walker said: 'We know from research that many drivers see cyclists as a separate subculture to which they don't belong.

'I hope drivers realise they are making assumptions about cyclists based on their appearance.

'If as a result of this study there were less injuries on the roads, that would be wonderful.'

Despite his findings, cyclists who wear helmets are more likely to survive a collision with a car, so the increased risk of an accident could be outweighed by the chances of living through it.

*1 inch = 2.5 centimetres

4 Journalists often start a newspaper article with the main topic to attract the reader's attention. In the article on the opposite page the main topic is given in the first sentence. What do the next two sentences do? Match the sentences with the functions.

Sentence 2   gives contrasting information.
Sentence 3   gives more details about the main topic.
              gives a reason for the behaviour described in the main topic.

5 Read the article carefully and find out more details about the research. Complete the chart.

Who carried out the research?	Dr Ian Walker, a traffic psychologist
Where?	
How?	
Why?	

6 Complete the sentences which summarize the main points of the article.

a Overtaking drivers get closer to cyclists who _wear helmets._
b They think these cyclists are _____
c Drivers give more space to _____
d _____ get closer to cyclists than other vehicles.
e In 2005 the number of cyclists who died in road accidents in Britain _____
f More people have started cycling to _____
g Cyclists who wear helmets have a better chance of _____

7 Do any of the main points surprise you?

8 Do you think cyclists should stop wearing helmets? Why? / Why not?

Focus on ...
synonyms

Complete this sentence from the article. The two missing words are synonyms – they have the same or a similar meaning.
Although road _____ generally have fallen to a record low, cyclist _____ rose by an alarming ten per cent last year, official casualty figures revealed in June.

The following words are all in the article. Circle the words in each list which are synonyms.
a cyclists   motorists   riders
b hit   struck   injured
c overtaking   carrying out   passing
d room   space   boom
e data   perception   thought
f suspected   rose   increased
g test   experiment   risk
h caution   collision   accident

Find the remaining words in the article and try and work out a synonym for each one. (Synonyms for some of them are in the article.)
a _motorists – drivers_
b _____
c _____
d _____
e _____
f _____
g _____
h _____

Can-do checklist

Tick what you can do.

	Can do	Need more practice
I can identify newspaper sections and articles from these sections.	✓	✓
I can read a newspaper selectively.		
I can find the main points in a newspaper article.		

A Are these statements true (T) or false (F)?

1 You should read every word of a text in order to find the information that you are looking for. ...... (Unit 1)
2 We sometimes scan a text to find a particular word, and then read the text around the word. ...... (Unit 2)
3 You should always approach a text as if you were reading it in the real world. ...... (Unit 3)
4 When we skim a text, we read every word. ...... (Unit 4)
5 We can use a variety of reading skills to read the same piece of text. ...... (Unit 5)
6 Texts are easier to understand if you know nothing about the topic before you begin to read. ...... (Unit 6)
7 Magazine articles usually begin by setting the scene and providing all the background information. ...... (Unit 7)
8 A newspaper headline usually summarizes the main point of the article. ...... (Unit 8)

B Now read the *Learning tips* for Units 1–8 on pages 87–9. Do you want to change any of your answers in Exercise A?

C Skim Texts A–D on the opposite page. Decide which text each of these people would read. Write the letter of the text(s) in the box.

9 someone who has been out all day and has just got home [ ]
10 someone who is planning a holiday abroad [ ]
11 someone who wants to make a hot drink [ ]
12 someone who is returning home after studying in Britain [ ]

D Read Texts A1 and A2 and tick ✓ the correct boxes in the chart.

		Cocoa powder	Drinking chocolate
13	This product already contains sugar.		
14	This product weighs less than the other.		
15	You need more of this product to make a drink.		
16	You need to use some cold milk to make this drink.		
17	This product costs less.		

E Read Text B. Complete these sentences.

18 .... people use mountain bikes in New Zealand than touring bikes.
19 You .... always borrow a bike from the hostel you're staying in.
20 If you want a bike for three or four weeks, it's .... expensive to rent than to buy.
21 Cyclists in New Zealand .... wear a helmet.
22 A cycle shop may give you back .... the amount you paid for a bike at the end of your trip.

F Carlos has contacted Excess Baggage PLC about transporting his baggage to Spain. Read Text C and decide if these sentences are true (T) or false (F).

23 This company transports baggage only to countries in Europe. ......
24 Carlos's baggage may travel by lorry to Spain. ......
25 If his baggage is very heavy, it is probably better to send it by road or ship. ......
26 He won't have to pay extra to use the company's packaging. ......
27 If Carlos can't lift one of his packages, it probably weighs more than the maximum allowed. ......

G Read Text D and put events a–e in order.

28 [ ] 29 [ ] 30 [ ] 31 [ ] 32 [ ]

a Tom read the electricity meter and completed the back of the card.
b Tom came home and saw the card that had been left.
c Tom went off to college the following morning.
d Tom put the card in the window near the front door.
e On 29 June someone came to check how much electricity Tom had used.

Text A1

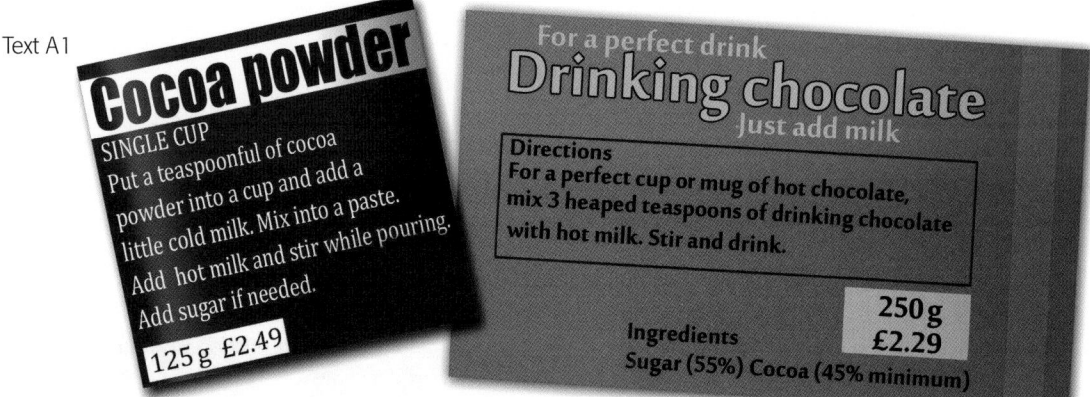

Cocoa powder

SINGLE CUP
Put a teaspoonful of cocoa powder into a cup and add a little cold milk. Mix into a paste. Add hot milk and stir while pouring. Add sugar if needed.

125 g £2.49

Text A2

For a perfect drink
Drinking chocolate
Just add milk

Directions
For a perfect cup or mug of hot chocolate, mix 3 heaped teaspoons of drinking chocolate with hot milk. Stir and drink.

250 g
£2.29

Ingredients
Sugar (55%) Cocoa (45% minimum)

Text B

CYCLING IN NEW ZEALAND

For those who are reasonably fit, cycling is a great way to see the countryside. Most people choose mountain bikes, but as most of the riding is on roads, touring bikes are equally good. If you just want to do a bit of local exploration, some hostels and guest houses have bikes you can use free of charge (or for a very small charge). Renting bikes for more than a day here and there can be expensive ($15–$35 a day).

It's probably cheaper to buy a bike if you're planning some long-distance cycle-touring. Look for bargains on hostel noticeboards (between $150 and $300 is a good deal). You'll often be able to pick up extras, like wet-weather gear, lights, helmet and a pump, reasonably too. (Note that helmets are required by law.) The advantage of buying from a cycle shop is that sometimes they will guarantee to buy back the bike at the end of your trip for about 50% of what you paid for it.

Text C

THE EXCESS BAGGAGE SERVICE

At Excess Baggage PLC, we can send your belongings to just about anywhere in the world. After all, we've been doing this for 20 years, and we are now the largest independent baggage forwarder in Europe.

SEA OR AIR WORLDWIDE?

We can send your baggage by sea or by air. We also offer a road freight service to many destinations in Europe. For some destinations, it may be more cost effective to send your belongings by air, even for larger quantities. The cost of sending goods via sea freight or road freight is determined by the volume (space taken up by your baggage). The cost of sending goods via air freight is determined by either the size or weight of your belongings, whichever is greater.

PACKING ADVICE & LIMITATIONS

You can pack your belongings into your own bags and suitcases or we can supply you with export-strength cartons and packaging for a nominal fee. Please note that no package should weigh more than 30–35 kilos, in accordance with UK Health & Safety Regulations. A good indication of this is if you can lift and carry these packages yourself.

Text D

Southern Electric

Date 29-6
Time ....

Call back

Dear Customer,
I called on behalf of your supplier today to:

- [x] **Read the electricity meter**
- [ ] **Read the gas meter**
- [ ] **Read the gas meter and electricity meters**
- [ ] **Inspect your meter**

I will be in the area again on the day marked below and hope to call back sometime before 8pm Monday to Friday and before 5pm on Saturday.

- [ ] **Today**
- [x] **Tomorrow**
- [ ] **This Saturday**
- [ ] **Monday**

If I need to read your meter and you do not want me to disturb you when I call back, please enter your readings on the back of this card and leave it where I will be able to see it. Thank you.

For meter inspections I will need access to your meter.

Providing a service on behalf of your supplier

H Skim the magazine article and answer the question.

33 What is it mainly about? Tick ✓ one of the boxes.
  a learning some typical Australian words ☐
  b finding somewhere to live in Sydney ☐
  c beginning a new job in Sydney ☐

New beginning

Down Under newbie Amanda Hemmings discovers that there's more to settling in to life in Australia than donning thongs and working on that tan

ONLY four weeks after landing on Australian soil I'm feeling like a true Sydneysider. I've become accustomed to saying 'capsicum' instead of red pepper, 'thongs' when I really mean flip flops, 'doona' for duvet (not that I've had a need for one yet) and I even caught myself saying 'no worries' the other day. With a few long hours spent relaxing on the beach, I'm even becoming less pommy white and more sun-kissed beach babe; well, almost.

Yes, the new Antipodean lifestyle suits me down to the ground. However, things weren't looking quite so rosy a couple of weeks ago when I was living out of a suitcase and eating stale hotel cornflakes.

Like most new arrivals, the quest to find a place to live became top priority. My boyfriend Mark and I wanted easy transport to the city, good cafés and bars, but more importantly to be a walk from the beach. Bondi was an obvious option, but after a visit we decided to avoid Sydney's backpacker capital. We went online (www. domain.com.au and www.justlisted.com.au are good starting points) and discovered that Coogee in the eastern suburbs fitted the bill perfectly.

Armed with the *Sydney Morning Herald* (Saturday's edition is good for rental accommodation), we set off to find our dream pad. But that dream soon turned into a nightmare. Firstly, we had 'arrived at the wrong time of year' as every agent brightly informed us. Apparently, mid-summer is not a good time to find rental properties, when ten couples will be fighting over one flat. Plus only unfurnished apartments are available in this city; not great news when you only plan to stay for a few months and have arrived with little more than a few bikinis and a jar of Marmite. Buying everything from sofas to saucepans hadn't even occurred to us; but this wasn't to be our only obstacle. 'A steady job would be an advantage,' beamed agent after agent. Arrgghhh! A bit of an issue for two travellers fresh off the plane, with no work lined up.

We soon turned into veteran flat-hunters and learnt a few tricks along the way. Apartments described as 'original-style' means old and crumbling, and 'cosy' is the generous term for broom cupboard. Be warned: agents have a tendency to be very imaginative with their details. However, unlike London, Sydney generally has good value rental properties, with a two-bed flat starting at around A$360 (about £148) a week, and the added bonus is that there's no council tax to pay. We also discovered a useful top tip: Australia Post will hold mail marked 'Poste Restante' for at least a month at any Post Office or agency. This comes in very handy if you're flat-hunting and have no fixed abode.

When we did eventually find a flat, things didn't get any easier. It's not a case of simply signing on the dotted line; there's a long-winded application process to go through. Securing a place to live in this city is no easy task. But we did it, and now with suitcases finally unpacked and the new Ikea furniture arranged, we have our dream apartment with a sea view (if on tiptoes).

I **Read the article again. Which four sentences about Amanda and Mark are true? Write the letters in the boxes in alphabetical order.**

34 ☐ 35 ☐ 36 ☐ 37 ☐

a They arrived in Australia four weeks ago.
b They stayed in a hotel before they found a flat.
c They decided to look for jobs first of all.
d They really wanted to live near the city centre.
e They decided to look for a flat in Bondi.
f They looked at advertisements in a newspaper.
g They moved into the flat as soon as they found it.
h They bought some new furniture for their flat.

J **Circle the best way to complete each sentence according to the text.**

38 They had arrived 'at the wrong time of year', which meant that *there weren't any cheap flats / lots of people were looking for accommodation*.

39 The problem if you 'only plan to stay a few months' is that *agents don't like very short rentals / you don't want to have to buy furniture*.

40 It's easier to get a flat if *you're working / you have money for a deposit*.

41 The flats they saw *were / weren't* always exactly as they were described in the advertisements.

42 The main advantage of flats in Sydney, compared with flats in London, was their *price / size*.

43 They *couldn't / were able to* receive mail while they were flat-hunting.

K **Which two sentences best summarize Amanda and Mark's experiences? Write the letters in the boxes.**

44 They ☐
a loved the hotel they were staying in.
b wish they'd never left London.
c are enjoying their new life in Australia.

45 Finding a flat ☐
a wasn't easy, but they've done it and they're pleased.
b was no more difficult than they expected.
d wasn't easy, and they're not particularly pleased with what they've got.

L **Below are two accommodation advertisements that Amanda and Mark looked at. Based on what you have already read about their search for accommodation, decide which flat they chose to rent. Give three reasons for your answer.**

46 I think they decided to rent flat ....
47 because ....
and in the text ....
48 because ....
and in the text ....
49 because ....
and in the text ....

A

One-bedroom second-floor unfurnished apartment. Suitable for couple or two singles. Attractive sunroom that could be used as a second bedroom or study. Gas kitchen and tidy bathroom with separate shower and bath. Near park, transport and tennis club, and only a short walk from Coogee beach. Minimum 3 months A$350 pw + utilities. Month by month also available at higher rent.

B

Huge ground-floor older style two-bedroom unit situated in a well-maintained block. Separate lounge and dining, kitchen with electric cooking, fridge, microwave, etc. Use of garden, with bbq area and clothes line. Close to public transport and the heart of Coogee. Professional couple with permanent positions only. A$500 pw, available end of December.

M **Which advertisement do these sentences refer to? Tick ✓ one of the boxes.**

50 This advertisement doesn't say if there's a telephone.
A ☐ B ☐ A and B ☐

51 This advertisement doesn't say how big the accommodation is.
A ☐ B ☐ A and B ☐

52 This advertisement doesn't say when you can move in.
A ☐ B ☐ A and B ☐

53 This advertisement doesn't say if there's a balcony.
A ☐ B ☐ A and B ☐

54 This advertisement doesn't say if bills are included.
A ☐ B ☐ A and B ☐

55 This advertisement doesn't say what the building is like.
A ☐ B ☐ A and B ☐

Get ready to read

○ (Circle) the words in these sentences about safety at work so that they are true for your workplace, or a workplace you are familiar with.

There *is / isn't* a lot of dangerous machinery that people use.

People *wear / don't wear* earplugs to protect themselves from noise.

The temperature *often / never* becomes unbearably hot or cold.

There *are / aren't* chemicals that can catch fire.

○ Fire is a danger in all workplaces. Read the sentences about what to do if you discover a large fire and complete them with words from the box.

> brigade   exit   alarm   drill

Sound the fire (a) .... to tell everyone there is a fire. Call the fire (b) ....

Follow the fire (c) .... and leave the building through a fire (d) ....

○ Match these compound nouns with the pictures.

a fire door 2   b fire engine ☐   c fire escape ☐   d fire extinguisher ☐   e fire hose ☐   f fire station ☐

go to Useful language p. 84

A Help prevent fire

1 You are going to read a leaflet about fire safety at work. How can a workplace be protected from fire? Write three more ways.

Don't leave piles of rubbish on the floor.

----

2 Scan the leaflet on the opposite page. Does it mention the three ways you suggested?

3 Match the beginnings with the endings to make sentences.

a If you smoke,

b Replace damaged cables

c Always keep corridors clear

d If there is a fire drill,

e Keep the office tidy

1 because waste paper can spread fire.

2 you must do so outdoors.

3 so that people can leave the building easily.

4 because they can cause electric shocks and fires.

5 go to your assembly point.

4 Match the sentences in Exercise 3 with the pictures in the leaflet. Write the numbers in the boxes.

a 3   b ☐   c ☐   d ☐   e ☐

Help prevent fire

Fire is always a threat, but you can help prevent it.

Use lighting and heaters safely

Make sure nothing that could burn is too close to lamps or heaters. Make sure that radiant parts on heaters are not exposed.

Respect electricity

It can cause shocks and fires. Do not use a damaged lead or plug. If required, turn off electrical appliances when leaving them unattended.

Clean up clutter

Rubbish may help start a fire or make a small fire bigger.

Take care with smoking materials

Smoking is not allowed on these premises. If you do smoke, smoke outside the building and only where it is allowed. Dispose of all matches and cigarette butts carefully in metal containers.

Store combustible materials safely

Don't keep them on escape routes, staircases or underneath enclosed staircases.

Don't block fire exits, escape routes or alarm call points

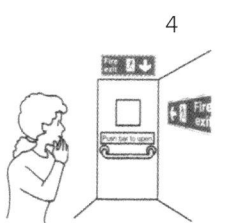

Make sure fire exits are free from obstructions and are not locked, chained or bolted.
Don't leave large items in corridors, or near staircases, or in front of alarm call points.

Keep all fire doors shut

Never wedge them open.

Know the fire drill

Learn in advance:

- the location and operation of the nearest fire exit and alternative exits
- what you should do when you hear the fire alarm
- your assembly point in case you need to leave the building

---

5 Four of the compound nouns with *fire* from *Get ready to read* are in the text. Scan the text and find them. What is each one? Use a dictionary if you need to.

1 A fire exit is a special door that people use to leave the building if there is a fire.

2 ....

3 ....

4 ....

Learning tip

Dictionaries – both bilingual and monolingual – are very useful when you are learning a language. However, try not to use them too much. When you are reading, try to work out the meaning of an unknown word. Think about the other words around it, the word class it belongs to (e.g. noun, verb), similar words you know in English and similar words in your own language. Then use the dictionary to check that you have worked out the meaning of the word correctly.

---

6 Find these words in the leaflet and try to work out their meaning. Then check your answers in a dictionary. Remember to check the pronunciation of the words too.

radiant plug electrical appliances
premises dispose combustible
obstructions wedge

Class bonus

In pairs, discuss fire safety at workplaces you know. Are these places safe? What could be done to make them safer? Write a list of points in English.

B Fire safety procedures

1 Skim the notice on the right. Add one of these words to the title.

> alarm brigade door drill exit

2 Read the sub-headings. Can you work out the meanings of *suspect* and *intermittent*?

3 The text mentions an 'alarm call point' and an 'assembly point'? What are these? What does *point* mean in these expressions?

----

4 Read the whole text and <u>underline</u> any words you don't understand. Then read the text again carefully and try to work out the meaning of these words. Remember to use the strategies in the *Learning tip* on page 47.

Did you know ...?

If you need to phone for the Fire Brigade in the UK, you can call 999 or 112. These are also the numbers for the other Emergency Services – police and ambulance. 112 is used throughout the European Union. Emergency numbers in other English-speaking countries are:

USA	911
Canada	911
Australia	000
New Zealand	111
South Africa	112

Fire

If you discover a fire or see smoke and suspect there is a fire

1 Shout 'FIRE!' to warn people in the immediate vicinity.

2 Sound the alarm by breaking the glass at the nearest alarm call point.

3 Go to Reception and report to the Person in Control, or to the Fire Brigade and Rescue Services when they arrive.

If you are in the building and hear the intermittent fire alarm

1 Continue working but be prepared to leave the building should the continuous alarm sound. Close all windows.

2 Do not use the lifts when you are moving around the building.

If you are in the building and hear the continuous fire alarm

1 Leave the building by the nearest exit not affected by the fire. If you are responsible for any visitors, ensure they leave with you and attend assembly point G. Those with mobile telephones should take them with them. Do not stop to collect personal belongings, coats, bags, etc.

2 Those in charge of departments or their deputies should briefly search their areas to ensure that the immediate vicinity is clear of staff and visitors.

3 When vacating the building, do not use the lifts.

4 Go to your assembly point.

5 Departmental heads or their deputies should ensure that all members of staff are accounted for.

6 If you believe anyone to be unaccounted for, report this to the Person in Control.

Assembly points
G Ground floor staff and visitors
1 First floor staff
2 Second floor staff
3 Third floor staff

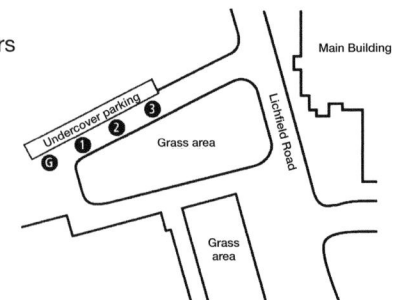

5 Read the first two sets of instructions and choose the correct answers.

a If you see a fire, you should
  1 shout 'Fire!' to the people who are near you. ☐
  2 run around the building shouting 'Fire!' ☐
  3 shout 'Fire!' to people outside in the street. ☐
b When you break the glass of the alarm call point, you
  1 make the fire alarm stop. ☐
  2 make the fire alarm ring. ☐
  3 make the fire alarm sound louder. ☐
c If the intermittent alarm sounds, you should
  1 use the stairs instead of the lift. ☐
  2 leave the building. ☐
  3 turn off your computer. ☐
d You should close all windows
  1 so that nobody can get into the building. ☐
  2 so that the noise won't disturb people outside. ☐
  3 so that air can't get in and spread the fire. ☐

Focus on ...
compound nouns

A compound noun consists of two nouns, for example, *fire alarm*. Here are six compound nouns which begin with *fire*. These compound nouns are written as one word. Match the words with the definitions.

firearm   firefighter   fireplace   firewall   firewood   ~~firework~~

a a small object that explodes to produce a loud noise and bright colours ___firework___
b someone whose job is to put out fires _____
c a gun that you can carry easily _____
d wood that is used for burning on a fire _____
e a space in the wall of a room where you can have a fire, or the structure around this space _____
f a system that stops other people looking at information on your computer while it is connected to the Internet _____

6 Read the third set of instructions. What should you do if you hear the continuous fire alarm in these situations?

a Your desk is on the ground floor, and you are having a meeting at your desk with two people from another company.
  You should ensure your visitors leave with you and you should go to assembly point G.
b You work on the first floor.
  _____
c Your mobile phone is in the top drawer of your desk.
  _____
d You are playing tennis after work, and your sports bag is under your desk.
  _____
e You are head of your department. Everyone in your department has left their desks and you are getting ready to leave.
  _____
f You are acting as head of your department. You are at your assembly point.
  _____
g When you get to the assembly point, you can't see one of your colleagues.
  _____

E✗tra practice
This unit has been about fire in the workplace. Go to www.firekills.gov.uk and click on Fire safety advice. Read the webpage Check your home and follow the advice. How safe is your home?

Can-do checklist

Tick what you can do.

	Can do	Need more practice
I can work out the meaning of unknown words from the context.		
I can understand a leaflet about preventing a fire.		
I can follow instructions for a fire drill.		

go to Useful language p. 85

Get ready to **read**

- ⊙ Circle the words in these sentences so that they are true for you.
  I would rather *speak / write* to someone than *speak / write* to them.
  My preferred method of communicating in writing is *by email / by letter.*
  I get *over / fewer than* 50 emails every day.
  I always try to respond to an email *the same day / within a few days.*
  I *am on some / am not on any* email mailing lists.

- ⊙ How do you organize your emails? Write *Y* (yes) or *N* (no).
  Do you put them in different folders? ......
  Do you delete them regularly? ......
  Do you keep printed copies of your emails? ......
  Do you copy them into your To Do list or calendar? ......

A I copied you in

Learning tip

When you read an email, find out who it is from and who it is for. Sometimes the message is just for you, sometimes it is for you as a member of a group, and sometimes you are copied in (cc = carbon copy, i.e. you are sent a copy of an email which has been sent primarily to someone else). If you know who the email has been sent to, you will know whether you have to reply, or take some kind of action.

1 Isabel Senna and Emma Wright both work for Bishops in Wellington, New Zealand. Isabel has received emails a–c. Who are they from and who are they to? Circle the names.

2 Why has Isabel been sent emails a–c? Match the emails with their purpose.

Email a	requests something.
Email b	makes a suggestion.
Email c	gives some information.

3 What exactly is the request, the suggestion and the information in emails a–c?

---

a ⊖ ⊖ ⊖

From: Emma Wright
To: Isabel Senna, Dan Vettori
cc:
Date/time: 11/10 9.25
Subject: Meeting with Jane cancelled
***
Isabel and Dan
Jane has just called to say that she is off sick today and won't be able to meet you both this afternoon. She sends her apologies. She probably won't be back in now until next week. Thanks,
Emma

b ⊖ ⊖ ⊖

From: Rotha Lim
To: Emma Wright, Isabel Senna
cc: Ben Parker
Date/time: 11/10   11.15
Subject: Conference folders
***
Hi there
Would you be available one day next week? Marketing have asked for help with making conference folders and getting things ready to be shipped to Wanaka before the beginning of November. If you work together, it should only take one afternoon. Let me know which and I'll try to join you.
Rotha

c ⊖ ⊖ ⊖

From: Dan Vettori
To: Isabel Senna
cc:
Date/time: 11/10   14.05
Subject: Meeting with Jane
***
Isabel
If Jane's back, is next Tuesday any good for you? Morning or afternoon, I don't mind. I'm off to Auckland on Wednesday with Greg for three days, so would prefer to meet before then.
Dan

Class bonus

Write Isabel's reply email to either Rotha or Dan. Then find someone who has written the other reply and exchange emails. Respond to the email you have received from this person.

Did you know ...?

Wellington is the capital of New Zealand. It is at the southern end of North Island. Wanaka is a lakeside resort town in the south of South Island.

4 Read emails d–f quickly. Who are they from and who are they to? Circle the names.

5 Why do you think Isabel has been copied in on emails d–f? Write sentences.

Email d She has been copied in so that she knows Paul, Rotha, Greg, Jane and Dan are aware that she will do anything urgent the following week.

Email e ....
....

Email f ....
....
....

d

From: Emma Wright
To: Paul Collingwood, Rotha Lim, Greg Kawana,
    Jane Reed, Dan Vettori
cc: Isabel Senna
Date/time: 11/10   14.40
Subject: Holiday next week
_____

Dear Team
I am out of the office next week, but will be back on 22 October. If you had anything you wanted me to do next week that can be done now, please let me know.
Isabel has kindly agreed to cover anything urgent while I'm away.
Emma

Focus on ...
collocations

A collocation is the combination of two or more words which often go together, for example, *send (my / his,* etc.) *apologies, working lunch.*

Find three verbs which go with the noun *meeting* in emails a–f. Use them to complete these sentences.
a You .... a meeting if you say that it will not happen.
b You .... a meeting if you arrange it for a certain time.
c You can .... a meeting if you say that it will happen at a later time.

Find two other collocations with *meeting* and complete these sentences.
d Isabel will bring the food to the ....
....
e The .... will take place on 16 October.

e

From: Emma Wright
To: Paul Collingwood
cc: Isabel Senna
Date/time: 11/10   15.15
Subject: Lunch for Monday
_____

Paul
I have managed to book lunch for Monday 15th.
They are providing a working lunch of sandwiches, crisps and fruit for six people along with water and orange juice. The food has to be collected at 11.45 from the canteen. I have asked Isabel to do that for you. She will bring it to your meeting room.
Thanks
Emma

f

From: Emma Wright
To: Jane Reed, Rotha Lim, Greg Kawana
cc: Paul Collingwood, Isabel Senna
Date/time: 11/10   15.50
Subject: Team meeting postponed
_____

Dear all
The team meeting scheduled for next Monday morning has been postponed. It will now take place next Tuesday (16 October), at 11.00 am, in Meeting Room 2. I won't be there, but Isabel will attend.
Thanks
Emma

6 Email f doesn't say why the team meeting has been postponed. Which of the other emails suggests a possible reason? What is it?

....

7 What do you learn about the team Isabel works with? Who is doing what next week?

B Leaving and joining

1 Read the email and then match a–c with the correct names.

		Emma
a	It's from	Greg
		Dan
b	It's to	Isabel
		Jane
c	It's about	Paul
		Rotha

From: Paul Collingwood
To: Jane Reed, Rotha Lim, Greg Kawana, Dan Vettori, Isabel Senna
cc:
Date/time: 6/11 10.45
Subject: Emma Wright

Dear Colleagues
It is with mixed emotions that I pass on this news – Emma has resigned!
She is leaving us to take up a job with Lynams in Napier. Her last day in the office will be the 17th (next Friday). I know Emma will be missed by all of us at Bishops who have worked closely with her over the last three years, but at the same time I can understand that this is a wonderful opportunity. I am sure that Emma will thoroughly enjoy the challenge her new job offers.
All best wishes
Paul

2 How does Paul feel about the news? Tick ✓ one of the boxes.

a He is happy that Emma is leaving. ☐
b He is sorry that she is leaving. ☐
c He is pleased for Emma, but sorry. ☐

3 Circle the correct words in these sentences.

a Emma's new job is with another *company / department.*
b She is leaving *at the end of the next week / in a week's time.*
c She has worked for the company *for three years / since Paul joined.*

4 Read the notice that Paul puts on the office noticeboard. Match the paragraphs with topics a–e.

a her personal qualities ☐
b the positions Emma has had ☐
c the announcement ☐1
d good wishes for the future ☐
e the work she has done ☐

5 Read the notice again and answer the questions.

a What is Emma's current job title?

----

b What does she do in her current job?

----

c What other positions has she had at Bishops? ------------------------------

d What is her new job going to be?

E✗tra practice

Are there any notices in English on the noticeboard where you work or study? If not, where can you find notices in English in your town / city? What are they about?

Date: 8 November

¹ Emma Wright is leaving Bishops to take up the role of Recruitment Administrator at Lynams in Napier. Her last day in the office is Friday 16 November.

² Emma has been working with us for more than three years. She started as a temporary keyboard operator on a six-month contract and then took on a permanent position as an administration assistant. Eighteen months ago she was promoted to the position of Office Administrator.

³ Emma has fantastic computer skills and under her direction we now know our PCs much better than we used to! Emma excelled herself in setting up a superb website, which has proved immensely successful. She has also updated the database on a regular basis, and taken over responsibilities for publicity and producing promotional items such as pens and notepads.

⁴ Emma is an invaluable member of the team and we will miss her enthusiasm and good humour greatly. Over the years Emma has been a tremendous friend and colleague to many of us here in Wellington and a welcome point of contact for our customers and suppliers.

⁵ I am sure you will want to join me in wishing her every success in her new career.

Paul Collingwood
Project & Development Manager

6 Look at this list of typical events that can take place when someone leaves a job. What usually happens in your country? Tick ✓ one or more of the boxes.

a The person who is leaving provides cakes. ☐
b Colleagues provide cakes. ☐
c Everyone signs a card for the person who is leaving. ☐
d The staff give money and buy a present for the person who is leaving. ☐
e There is a small leaving party in the office and the boss makes a speech. ☐
f People all go out for a drink or a meal with the person who is leaving. ☐

7 Read the email from Emma and <u>underline</u> the events in Exercise 6 which are true for her.

Emma Wright

To:	Paul Collingwood, Jane Reed, Rotha Lim, Greg Kawana, Dan Vettori
	10/11 14.00
cc:	Isabel Senna
Subject:	Leaving do

Dear Friends and Colleagues

As you know, I'm leaving next week and moving away from Wellington. There will be coffee and cakes (which my mum has baked) at 4.30 pm next Friday in the coffee area. Also, Isabel has booked a table at my favourite Chinese restaurant (Uncle Chang's, 72 Courtenay Place), for 7.30 that evening. Please let her know if you can come along. Everyone is welcome!

I know some of you will be at the Sales Conference in Wanaka next week. If I don't see you before I go, take care and thanks for being such good colleagues these last three years!

Best wishes
Emma

---

8 Read another notice that Paul has put on the noticeboard. Is someone else leaving Bishops? Who is Vincent Ingram?

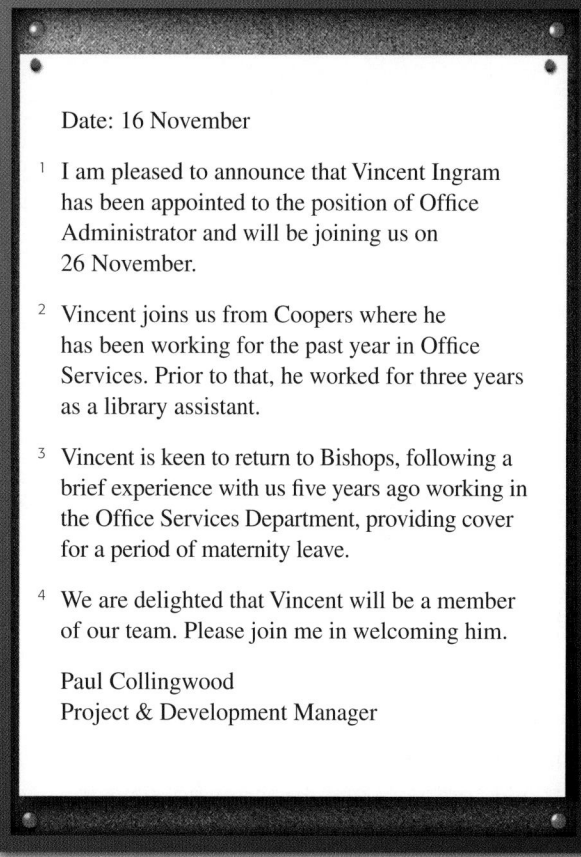

Date: 16 November

1 I am pleased to announce that Vincent Ingram has been appointed to the position of Office Administrator and will be joining us on 26 November.

2 Vincent joins us from Coopers where he has been working for the past year in Office Services. Prior to that, he worked for three years as a library assistant.

3 Vincent is keen to return to Bishops, following a brief experience with us five years ago working in the Office Services Department, providing cover for a period of maternity leave.

4 We are delighted that Vincent will be a member of our team. Please join me in welcoming him.

Paul Collingwood
Project & Development Manager

9 Match functions a–d with the paragraphs in the notice about Vincent.

a giving information about work history — paragraph 1
b encouraging staff to welcome someone — paragraph 2
c announcing a change in personnel — paragraph 3
d describing previous in-house experience — paragraph 4

10 Do you think Vincent will enjoy working at Bishops? Why? / Why not?

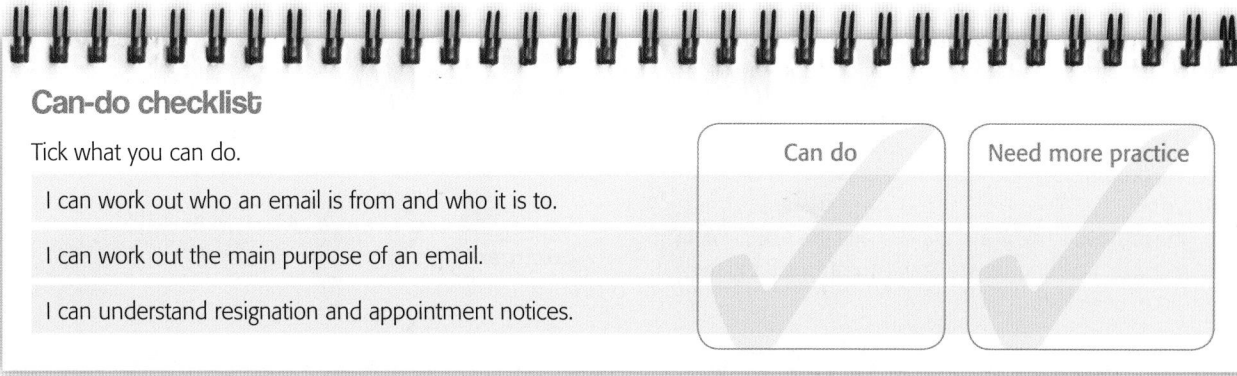

Can-do checklist

Tick what you can do.

	Can do	Need more practice
I can work out who an email is from and who it is to.		
I can work out the main purpose of an email.		
I can understand resignation and appointment notices.		

go to Useful language p. 85

Get ready to **read**

- Have you ever been asked to fill in a questionnaire? What was it about? Tick ✓ one or more of the boxes.

  something you had bought ☐   conditions at work ☐
  facilities or services in a town ☐   other (specify what) ....
  a holiday ☐

- If you wrote about the feedback from some questionnaires, which of these would you include? Tick ✓ one or more of the boxes.
  a a description of how you devised the questionnaire ☐
  b information about how long it took to devise ☐
  c an analysis of the feedback ☐
  d conclusions from the feedback ☐
  e recommendations for changes based on the feedback ☐
  f recommendations for future questionnaires ☐

A Holiday questionnaire

1 Ivana works for Mountain Travel, a British travel company that arranges holidays in Europe. As part of her job, she has to read feedback from clients about their holidays. Read the questionnaire on the opposite page and answer the questions.

a Which country did the client visit?
   Slovenia....

b Which areas did he visit?
   ....

c Which hotels did he stay in?
   ....

d Did he enjoy his holiday?
   ....

2 Which of these aspects of the holiday did the client particularly like? Tick ✓ one or more of the boxes.

a the bedroom at the Vila Orel ☐
b the breakfasts at the Vila Orel and the Hotel Bella Vista ☐
c the picnic lunches at the Vila Orel and the Turist Hotel ☐
d the welcome and service at the Turist Hotel and the Hotel Bella Vista ☐

Did you know ...?

Slovenia is a small country in south-eastern Europe to the east of Italy. It is one of the six republics that made up the former Yugoslavia. Much of the land is mountainous and is very good for walking; the highest mountain is Mount Triglav (2,863 m) in the Julian Alps in the north-west. The town of Kranjska Gora is a popular resort in both summer and winter. Bled, on the shore of Lake Bled, and Lake Bohinj also attract many walkers and skiers.

3 Look at the client's two comments about the hotels. Circle the correct words in these sentences.

a Comment 1 is *positive / negative*.
b Comment 2 is mainly *positive / negative*.

4 Underline the client's criticism in each comment.

RM	DR		ACT	CR		RESP

Mr B Drummond CF6 4UE

MOUNTAIN TRAVEL POST-HOLIDAY QUESTIONNAIRE

We are constantly working to maintain and improve all aspects of our service. Your comments are vital to us in this effort and are much appreciated. Please use our special FREEPOST address: Mountain Travel Ltd, FREEPOST, York Y03 7BT.

The Lakes & Julian Alps – a holiday in Slovenia

HOW WOULD YOU DESCRIBE YOUR OVERALL LEVEL OF SATISFACTION WITH YOUR HOLIDAY?

Please tick as applicable:

Very satisfactory ✓   Satisfactory ☐
Fairly satisfactory ☐   Unsatisfactory ☐

ACCOMMODATION

Please rate aspects of each hotel on a scale of 1 to 5, with 5 the highest score.

	Vila Orel (Kranjska Gora)	Turist Hotel (Lake Bohinj)	Hotel Bella Vista (Lake Bled)
Bedroom	5	3	4
Breakfast	5	4	5
Picnic Lunch	3	3	n/a
Welcome & service	4	3	3
Hotel Facilities	4	4	4

Do you have any other comments about the hotels?

(1) We had paid for picnic lunches in both the Vila Orel and the Turist Hotel – every day we got the same boring cheese roll. Would it not be possible for guests to make their own picnic from the breakfast buffet?
(2) The Vila Orel is very nice indeed. Its location near the river and at the foot of the mountains is something special. My only criticism is that there is no lift – the poor receptionist had to carry my suitcase up two flights of stairs!

TRAVEL

Please rate aspects of your travel arrangements on a scale of 1 to 5, with 5 as the highest score

FLIGHTS   **TRANSFERS**
Adria Airways [4]   Taxi Jager [4]
                         Taxi Pehta [4]

Each questionnaire is read by a member of our senior management and all comments are used to improve our holidays. Any negative comments will be particularly scrutinized and shared with hoteliers or other of our partners where appropriate.

Please tick this box only if you wish to receive a reply to the points you have raised on your questionnaire: ☐
You can expect a response within three weeks of your questionnaire arriving with us.

MANY THANKS FOR COMPLETING THIS QUESTIONNAIRE

5 What does Mountain Travel claim to do with any negative comments it receives? Tick ✓ one or more of the boxes.

a They consider any negative comments very carefully. ☐
b They always pass on negative comments to the hotel owners. ☐
c They always let the client know what they have done in response to his or her comment. ☐

6 What do you think Mountain Travel might do in connection with Mr Drummond's comments?

7 Look at some more clients' comments and decide if each one is mainly positive (P) or mainly negative (N). Then think about how Mountain Travel could deal with any negative comments.

a I understood that the Vila Orel was in Kranjska Gora – but it's 20 minutes' walk from the town. Walking there and back in the dark to the nearest restaurant is not my idea of fun! N

b Our holiday was at the end of September, so the hotels were quiet. My friend and I had booked a twin room. However, we each had a large double room in the attic at the Vila Orel. The rooms were wonderful! ......

c It's lovely to have the swimming pools at the Vila Orel and Turist Hotel – and to have them to yourselves! ......

d The Turist Hotel is in a very quiet location off the main road at the far end of the lake. Wouldn't it be possible to stay at the opposite end of the lake – in the village of Bohinj itself? I noticed the Hotel Julija there. It's very near the lake, and there are shops and things! ......

e The Hotel Bella Vista has wonderful gardens and a fantastic location. I don't recommend staying there on Saturday night, however! When we were there, a wedding party went on until five am. The music was incredibly loud and the receptionist didn't want to do anything about it! ......

Class bonus

Write some positive and negative comments about a hotel you have stayed in. Exchange your comments with a partner. As you read your partner's comments, imagine you are Ivana. Is each comment positive or negative? What – if anything – might you do about the negative comments?

B Report on questionnaire feedback

1 Ivana's boss has asked her to analyse the feedback from all the holiday questionnaires she received and to write a report on the findings. Skim her report and answer the questions.

a Which holiday is the report about?

----

b What is the main focus of the report?

----

2 Look at the first paragraph. In terms of the report, which is the more important number – 239 or 150?

3 How satisfied were the clients? Choose the correct words to make a sentence.

More than *a quarter / half / three-quarters* were *fairly satisfied / satisfied / very satisfied*.

4 Look at the chart in the report and answer the questions.

a Which aspect of which hotel was the most highly rated?
 the bedrooms at the Hotel
 Bella Vista (98%)

b Which aspect of which hotel was the lowest rated?

----

c Which hotel was most highly rated overall?

----

d Which aspect was the most highly rated overall?

----

5 <u>Underline</u> the four most common client criticisms mentioned in Ivana's report.

The Lakes and Julian Alps: feedback from holiday questionnaires

The Lakes and Julian Alps is one of our most popular holidays – there were 239 bookings during the summer season (a total of 506 clients). However, of the 239 questionnaires which were sent out to clients, only 150 were returned.

Overall satisfaction with the holiday was very high. Responses were as follows:

very satisfactory	116
satisfactory	33
fairly satisfactory	2*
unsatisfactory	0

* Both holidays were spoilt by poor weather. In addition, one group got food poisoning in a restaurant in Kranjska Gora.

Accommodation

Clients rate five aspects of each hotel, with a mark from 1 (minimum) to 5 (maximum). The results from 150 questionnaires give a minimum total of 150 and a maximum total of 750. The total mark for each aspect has been converted into a percentage of the maximum possible. For example: a total of 690 out of 750 = 92%. The results are:

	Vila Orel (Kranjska Gora)	Turist Hotel (Lake Bohinj)	Hotel Bella Vista (Lake Bled)
Bedroom	92%	49%	98%
Breakfast	81%	77%	94%
Picnic lunch	47%	42%	n/a
Welcome & service	81%	72%	88%
Facilities	81%	70%	88%

Aspects of the accommodation that were most criticised in clients' comments were:

- **Bedrooms at the Turist Hotel** These are a rather dull brown, but the manager assures us that the hotel will be refurbished this winter. In other words, the rooms will be totally redecorated and updated.
- **Picnic lunches provided by the Vila Orel and the Turist Hotel** These were criticised as being plain and boring. A suggestion was made that guests could make up their own picnic from the breakfast buffet. We have spoken to the managers of both hotels about the picnic lunches; whereas the Vila Orel is happy to adopt this scheme, the Turist Hotel would prefer to continue with the existing situation. I suggest that, in future, guests arrange their own lunches. As a result, we would no longer offer pre-payment for lunches as an option. Either guests can come to an arrangement with the hotel concerned, or they can buy lunch while they are out for the day. Eating out in Slovenia is cheap, and there are places to eat everywhere – even on walks in remote areas.
- **Noise from wedding parties at the Hotel Bella Vista** This can be loud enough to keep guests awake at night. Since most of our guests stay at the hotel on Saturday night, the best thing we can do is to warn clients in advance when they phone us to make their booking.
- **Remote location of the Turist Hotel** Several people suggested that a hotel in the village of Bohinj might be preferable to staying at the far end of the lake. However, there is a frequent bus service (every hour) from the Turist Hotel to Bohinj and then on to Bled; furthermore, the village of Bohinj can be noisy at night.

Transfers
No criticisms at all!

Learning tip

Make sure you know the meaning of words and expressions used to link facts and ideas. This will help you to understand the meaning of the text and what the writer is saying. Here are some examples:

giving a reason	*because, since, as*
expressing a contrast	*whereas, otherwise, but, while, however, although*
expressing a result	*consequently, therefore, as a result*
rephrasing	*in other words, i.e.*
giving an example	*for example, for instance, e.g.*
adding something	*furthermore, in addition, also*

6 Answer these questions about Ivana's responses to the criticisms. (Circle) any linking words and expressions in the report that help you answer the questions.

a When the rooms at the Turist Hotel are refurbished, what will happen to them?

----

b Are both hotels prepared to let guests choose their own picnic from the breakfast buffet?

----

c Why might Mountain Travel stop offering pre-payment for lunches as an option?

----

d Why should Mountain Travel warn people in advance about the noise from the wedding parties?

----

e Does Ivana want to offer a hotel in Bohinj instead of the Turist Hotel?

----

7 How do you think Ivana's boss will feel when she reads this report? Will she be pleased about the feedback?

Focus on ...
linking words

(Circle) the correct linking word or expression to complete this extract from the report.

> Several people suggested that a hotel in the village of Bohinj might be preferable to staying at the far end of the lake. *However / In addition / Consequently*, there is a frequent bus service from the Turist Hotel to Bohinj and then on to Bled.

Add a linking word or expression to each of these sentences before adding them to the end of the four bulleted paragraphs in the report. (The sentences are in the same order as the paragraphs.)

a .... , new lighting will be installed in each room.

b .... , on the walk from the Turist Hotel there is a café serving food just below the waterfall.

c .... , we could offer another hotel as an alternative to the Hotel Bella Vista for Saturday nights.

d .... , this alternative would solve one problem, but create another.

Extra practice

Look at the website www.realholidayreports.com and read some reviews of other hotels in Kranjska Gora, Bohinj and Bled. Click on Reports, then link to Eastern Europe, then Slovenia. Are the reviews positive or negative?

Can-do checklist

Tick what you can do.

	Can do	Need more practice
I can interpret a completed questionnaire.		
I can distinguish between comments and suggested action.		
I can understand how writers link facts and ideas.		

Get ready to read

- If you wanted to find a new job, which of the following would you do? Tick ✓ one or more of the boxes.
  Look at advertisements in newspapers or in shop windows. ☐
  Phone the Human Resources department of a company you'd like to work for. ☐
  Visit the website of a company you'd like to work for and look at the vacancies webpage. ☐
  Visit recruitment websites. ☐
  Register with a recruitment agency. ☐
  Speak to friends and family and ask them for help. ☐

- Have you ever applied for a job? How did you find it? Did you get the job?

- What are the main steps in getting a new job? Put these steps in the correct order.
  a You receive a letter inviting you to attend an interview. ☐
  b You accept the job offer. ☐
  c You see an advertisement for a job you're interested in. ☐1
  d You receive a letter or a phone call offering you the job. ☐
  e You send in your CV or you complete an application form. ☐
  f You attend the interview. ☐

go to Useful language p. 85

A I've seen an advert

1 Imagine you are studying in Dublin, Ireland. You see the advertisement on the opposite page. What is it for? Tick ✓ one of the boxes.
  a a job on the shop floor of a bookshop ☐
  b a job in the mail order department of a bookshop ☐
  c a job in the accounts department of a bookshop ☐

2 Read the advertisement again and answer as many of these questions as you can.
  a What is the title of the job?
    Part–time Administrator
  b Where exactly would you work?
    ----
  c What would you do?
    ----
  d How many hours would you work each week?
    ----
  e What time would you finish work each day?
    ----
  f How much would you get paid?

THE INTERNATIONAL BOOK SHOP
23–25 MEATH ROAD, DUBLIN 4

VACANCY
PART-TIME ADMINISTRATOR
20 HRS/WK – MORNINGS

We have a part-time vacancy in our Mail Order department at The International Book Shop. The shop is the premier international bookshop in Ireland and comprises a large range of books, magazines and newspapers, plus a growing Mail Order business.

Our Mail Order department is expanding rapidly and we are seeking to employ an administrator to handle orders, keep the database up-to-date and carry out general tasks related to customer orders. The role would be offered initially on a part-time basis. The required hours would cover 5 mornings a week with a 9 am start and would include Saturday mornings. There may be the option to become full time.

Applicants must have:
1 ■ Strong data input skills and familiarity with using spreadsheets, databases, email and word processing.
2 ■ Natural enthusiasm and a confident telephone manner.
3 ■ An understanding of the importance of attention to detail and accuracy.
4 ■ A methodical approach to tasks.
5 ■ A willingness to learn in a customer-focused environment.
6 ■ A willingness to take their own initiative.
A foreign language is desirable but not essential.

Deadline for applications: Wednesday 2nd August

To apply, please send in your CV to
Michael O'Grady, Manager, The International Book Shop, 23–25 Meath Road, Dublin 4

3 **Which of the sentences below describe you? Tick ✓ one or more of the boxes.**

a I can make decisions and do things without someone telling me what to do. ☐
b I plan my day's work in an ordered way. ☐
c I am keen to be involved and like talking to people. ☐
d I am motivated and enjoy finding out about new things. ☐
e I am careful to get everything exactly right. ☐

4 **Match the sentences in Exercise 3 with qualities listed in the advertisement. Write the numbers of the bullet points in the boxes.**

a 6   b ☐   c ☐   d ☐   e ☐

5 **You decide to apply for the job. How do you apply for it? When must you apply?**

---

6 **Pilar, a student in your class, also wants to apply for the job. Look at this part of her CV. Do you think Pilar is suitable for the job? Why? / Why not?**

Previous employment
1 Sales assistant   London   3 months
Main responsibilities: stocking shelves, selling goods, dealing with refunds.
Reasons for leaving: Summer job only – returned to Madrid for commercial course.

2 Personal Assistant   Madrid   2 years
Main responsibilities: office administration/correspondence, accounts and customer service.
Reasons for leaving: The business was sold, and I lost my job.

3 Tour guide   Madrid   6 months
Main responsibilities: showing groups of people around the city.
Reasons for leaving: I wanted to come to Dublin to study English.

Languages Spanish (mother tongue), English (proficient), French (intermediate)

7 **Would you be interested in this job? Why? / Why not?**

Class bonus
Think about a job you've had (or one that you would like). What skills and qualities did / would you need for it? Write a list. Don't include the job title. Exchange lists with another person. Try to guess your partner's job.

E✗tra practice
Look at the job advertisements section of a newspaper from your country. Are any of the advertisements in English? Do any of them mention that English is required? Do any of them mention which skills and qualities are desirable? Cut out an advertisement that interests you.

B Further to our telephone conversation

1 You are going to read a letter which uses formal language. First look at the pairs of words in *italics*. Circle the more formal alternative.

a *in* / *within* our company
b your *pay* / *salary* will be
c depends on *completion* / *finishing*
d 10 days' *holiday* / *leave*
e your *proposed* / *suggested* working hours
f *All the best,* / *Yours sincerely*, Michael O'Grady

2 Read the letter and tick ✓ the correct sentence.

a The letter is telling Pilar that she hasn't got the job at the bookshop. ☐
b The letter is offering Pilar the job at the bookshop. ☐
c The letter is repeating the job offer made over the phone. ☐

The International Book Shop
23–25 Meath Road
Dublin 4

tel: (00353) 1 249241
fax: (00353) 1 790061

Ms Pilar Morientes
76 Cork Place
Dublin 7

14 August 20__

Dear Ms Morientes

Re: Part-time Administrator

Further to our telephone conversation, I am delighted to confirm our offer of employment as Part-time Administrator within our organization.

The position is offered to you at a salary of £8,000 per annum and is subject to successful completion of the 13-week probationary period and receipt of satisfactory references.

1 Your normal working week will total 20 hours. Where it is necessary for you to work in excess of your normal hours, extra payment will be made.
2 Annual leave entitlement starts at 22 days per financial year and increases with service.
3 Your remuneration will be paid by direct credit transfer into a Bank / Building Society Account, on the last Friday of each calendar month.

Please would you confirm acceptance of this offer in writing as soon as possible, together with your proposed commencement date.

In the meantime, may I wish you every success in your future with our company.

Yours sincerely

Michael O'Grady

Michael O'Grady
Manager

Learning tip

Most of our everyday correspondence, such as notes and emails, is in informal language. However, on some occasions we receive formal letters. The language used in these is serious and correct, and less like spoken language. One way of understanding the content of a formal letter is to put it into more neutral everyday language.

Did you know ...?

Formal letters end *Yours sincerely* when the sender knows the person he / she is writing to, or knows the name of the person. When the sender doesn't know the name of the recipient, letters begin *Dear Sir or Madam* and end *Yours faithfully*.

3 Read the letter and find a more formal alternative for these words.

a work ..... employment .....
b job .....
c depends on .....
d more than .....
e start .....

4 Explain these parts of the letter in your own words.

a Further to our telephone conversation
We have already spoken on the phone and .....
b to confirm our offer
.....
c £8,000 per annum
.....
d 13-week probationary period
.....
e Annual leave entitlement
.....
f 22 days per financial year
.....
g increases with service
.....
h remuneration
.....

5 What does Pilar have to do if she wants the job?

.....
.....

Focus on ...
the layout of letters

Read these sentences about the layout of formal letters. Are the sentences true (T) or false (F)?

a The letterhead – the sender's business address, etc. – is at the top of the page. _T_
b The receiver's name and address are on the right. _____
c The date is below the receiver's address. _____
d The subject heading is under the salutation (*Dear* …). _____
e Formal letters are never typed. _____
f There is a space between each paragraph. _____
g There is no space before the first word of each paragraph. _____
h Letters end with a signature below the typed name and title. _____

Write Pilar's letter of acceptance. In your letter, make sure you:
- thank Michael O'Grady for the offer
- state your preferred start date
- say that you have booked a holiday in October.
Remember to lay out your letter in the correct way.

Can-do checklist

Tick what you can do.

	Can do	Need more practice
I can understand a job advertisement.		
I can distinguish between formal and informal language.		
I can understand an offer of employment and confirm acceptance.		

Get ready to read

- Match the industries with the icons.
  - a agriculture [4]
  - b chemicals [ ]
  - c financial and business services [ ]
  - d manufacturing [ ]
  - e petroleum [ ]
  - f tourism [ ]

- What are the main industries in your country or region? Write a list. Use the words above and any others.

----

go to Useful language p. 86

A Economic structure

1 Youssef, who works for a chemical company in the United States, is going on a business trip to Singapore. He decides to find out about Singapore's Gross Domestic Product – the total value of goods produced and services provided by the country in a year – on a website. Look at these tables from one of the webpages. Which of the tables mention GDP? Tick ✓ one or more of the boxes.

a [ ] b [ ] c [ ] d [ ]

Learning tip

We don't only read texts. We also read visuals, such as tables, graphs and diagrams. Often these are a more direct way of presenting information than through text. Visuals sometimes have to be read with text, but at other times they stand alone. As with texts, we always read them with a purpose and that is to extract meaning.

Economic structure of Singapore

a

	2002	2003	2004	2005
GDP at market prices (S$ bn)	158.4	161.5	181.7	194.4
GDP (US$ bn)	88.5	92.7	107.5	116.8
Real GDP growth (%)	4.0	2.9	8.7	6.4
Export of goods (US$ bn)	140.8	161.7	201.0	232.3
Exchange rate (S$: US$)	1.79	1.74	1.69	1.66
Population (m)	4.2	4.2	4.2	4.3

b

Origins of gross domestic product 2005	% of total
Manufacturing	26.8
Business services	12.6
Transport & communications	11.9
Financial services	10.8
Construction & utilities	3.6
Others	34.3

c

Principal exports 2005	US$ bn
Machinery & equipment	135.2
Petroleum products	27.6
Chemicals	26.2
Manufactured goods	10.5
Food	2.3

d

Main destinations of exports 2005	% of total
Malaysia	14.3
US	11.0
Hong Kong	10.1
China	9.3
Japan	5.9
Thailand	4.4
South Korea	3.8

2 Are these statements about Singapore's GDP true (T) or false (F)?

a GDP was worth just over 90 billion US dollars in 2002. ..F..

b GDP rose by less than three per cent in 2003. ......

c The GDP's rate of growth in 2004 was three times what it was in 2003. ......

d GDP increased by just under 9 billion US dollars in 2005. ......

e The manufacturing sector contributed the most to GDP in 2005. ......

f The transport and communications sector contributed more to GDP in 2005 than the business services sector. ......

g The contribution to GDP of the financial services sector was twice that of the construction and utilities sector in 2005. ......

3 Look at tables c and d on the opposite page. (Circle) the correct words in these sentences.

a The value of chemicals was *more* / *less* than the value of manufactured goods which were exported in 2005.

b Chemicals were the *third* / *second* biggest export in 2005.

c More goods were exported to the *US* / *Hong Kong* in 2005.

d Just *over* / *under* one tenth of Singapore's exports went to the US in 2005.

4 Youssef's company wants to export chemicals to Singapore, so he looks at some import figures. Look at visuals e–g on the webpage on the right. Complete the sentences with these terms.

pie chart   bar chart   line graph

Visual e is a ....
Visual f is a ....
Visual g is a ....

Did you know …?

The tiny island state of Singapore, south of Malaysia, is one of the world's most prosperous places. It has one of the busiest ports in the world and is the world's fourth largest foreign exchange trading centre.

5 Look again at both webpages and compare the information about imports and exports. (Circle) the correct phrase in each sentence. Sometimes you will need to look at one webpage and sometimes you will need to look at both.

a In 2005, Singapore imported *more than* /(*less than*)/ *the same amount as* it exported.

b The value of Singapore's imports between 2002 and 2005 *fell* / *rose* / *stayed the same*.

c In 2005, Singapore imported *more chemicals than* / *fewer chemicals than* / *the same quantity of chemicals as* it exported.

d In 2005, Singapore spent more on imported manufactured goods than it did on imported *machinery and equipment* / *food* / *crude petroleum*.

e In 2005, Singapore imported *more from China than* / *less from China than* / *about the same amount from China as* from Japan.

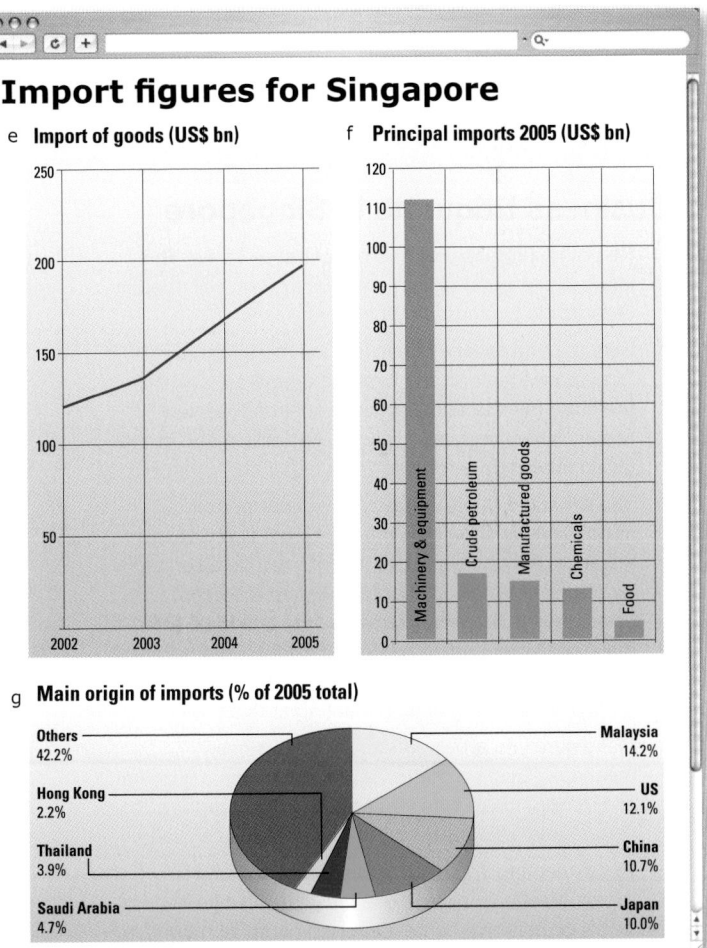

Import figures for Singapore

e **Import of goods (US$ bn)**

f **Principal imports 2005 (US$ bn)**

g **Main origin of imports (% of 2005 total)**

Others 42.2%
Hong Kong 2.2%
Thailand 3.9%
Saudi Arabia 4.7%
Malaysia 14.2%
US 12.1%
China 10.7%
Japan 10.0%

Class bonus

Find out about another country and its exports and imports on the *Economist* website www.economist.com/countries Write some sentences like those in Exercise 5. Exchange your sentences with a partner. Can you choose the correct word in your partner's sentences?

B Business etiquette

1 In the United States, there are certain ways of behaving at business meetings that are considered polite. Read this list of business etiquette instructions for the United States. Do people in your country do these things at business meetings? Tick ✓ one or more of the boxes.

a Always wear a jacket. ☐
b Arrive on time. ☐
c Greet people with 'Good morning / afternoon', or the equivalent. ☐
d Shake other people's hands firmly as a way of greeting. ☐
e Look other people in the eye to show interest and respect. ☐

2 Youssef wants to find out about business etiquette in Singapore, so he reads this webpage. Read it and find out if business people in Singapore do the things in Exercise 1. Write Y (yes) or N (no).

a N b ..... c ..... d ..... e .....

File   Edit   View   Favorites   Tools   Help

Address   Go   Links »

Business Etiquette in Singapore

1   Be polite, professional and patient at all times. This leads to the good relationships which you will need in order to do business in Singapore.

2   Bear in mind that business is done more formally in Singapore than in many Western countries, and that there are rules of etiquette that must be followed. Status is very important, and the eldest person in the group is always respected.

3   You will need to plan ahead. Whenever possible, appointments should be made at least two weeks in advance. Nowadays appointments can be arranged by phone or email, although writing to the person concerned is the most formal way to schedule a meeting. Many businesses close during Chinese New Year (late January / early February), so there is no point in even trying to fix a meeting at this time.

4   Make sure you arrive punctually for business meetings. This is a matter of respect. If you are going as a group, make sure you are lined up according to your status. Likewise, wait to be seated.

5   When meeting someone for the first time, and in formal meetings, always use the person's title and family or personal name. Only use personal names or nicknames when you are invited to do so, or when you have known someone for a long time.

6   Handshaking isn't part of Asian culture, so a handshake in Singapore is much softer and lighter to the touch than a Western one. Singaporeans don't understand the significance that Westerners give to a firm handshake.

7   Business cards are exchanged at the beginning of meetings and are always handed out so that the typeface faces the recipient. Protocol demands that you hold the card with both hands and examine it carefully; before putting the card into your card case, smile in order to show that you have noted who the other person is. This is a form of respect to that person and it reflects how the business relationship will be treated. Make sure your own business cards are in perfect condition before you hand them out.

8   Your Singaporean counterparts may not greet you with 'Good morning / afternoon / evening' or 'How are you?' Instead, you may be asked 'Have you eaten?' or 'Where are you going?'

9   Jackets do not normally have to be worn at meetings because of Singapore's hot and humid weather.

10 Before business discussions begin, there is often a period of small talk. Food, tourist attractions, the arts, music, and mutual friends are the safest topics.

11 As a sign of respect, Singaporeans don't always look people in the eye – especially if the person is older or has a higher status. Asian courtesy is very different from Western behaviour in this case, so don't be offended if this happens to you. Similarly, Singaporeans would not disagree with or question someone who is senior in rank.

3 What reasons does the webpage give for why Singaporeans do or don't follow the customs mentioned in Exercise 1? <u>Underline</u> the information on the webpage.

4 What should Youssef do when he receives a business card from someone he meets at a meeting in Singapore? Put the steps in order.

a look at the card carefully ☐
b take the card with both hands ☐1☐
c put the card in his card case ☐
d smile at the other person ☐

YĪN MÁRKETING PTE LTD

Kelvin Tan
29 Tuas Road #07-21
(65) 6321 9876
ktanyin@singnet.com.sg

5 Look at the steps in Exercise 4. Is this the way people exchange business cards in your country?

6 Here are some sentences which could be added to the end of some of the points on the webpage. Match the sentences with the points in the list. Write the numbers in the boxes.

File Edit View Favorites Tools Help
Address [   ] ▼ → Go Links »

a Take time to learn Asian etiquette, and to develop business contacts. ☐1☐
b People will take their seats in a strict order. ☐
c Wait for your Singaporean counterpart to offer you their hand for a handshake. ☐
d If you are meeting Chinese Singaporeans, you might consider having one side of your card translated into Mandarin. ☐
e You may need to encourage people to ask questions, so always make sure you smile when someone asks a question. ☐

7 How similar is business etiquette in Singapore to business etiquette in your country? What are the main similarities and differences?

Focus on ...
the passive infinitive

Complete these extracts from the webpage.

a there are rules of etiquette that must __be followed__
b appointments should _____ at least two weeks in advance
c appointments can _____ by phone or email

Find and underline five more examples of the passive infinitive in the text.

Complete these sentences with the passive infinitive of the verb in brackets.

d Don't _____ to take off your jacket. (embarrass)
e You have to _____ when to sit down. (tell)
f You may _____ to use personal names. (invite)
g You mustn't _____ before your boss. (introduce)
h You may _____ with a nod rather than a handshake. (greet)
i You will _____ to arrive on time for business meetings. (expect)

E✗tra practice

Read about business etiquette in your own country on the Internet. The website www.cyborlink.com may be able to help you. Do you agree with everything that you read? Have you learned anything you didn't know?

Can-do checklist

Tick what you can do.

	Can do	Need more practice
I can interpret statistics.		
I can interpret charts and graphs.		
I can find out about business etiquette in another country.		

○ Match the beginnings and endings of the sentences.
  a You can find facts about a large number of subjects in   a dictionary.
  b You can look up the meaning of a word in   a thesaurus.
  c You can look up synonyms for certain words in   an encyclopaedia.

○ Which dictionary would you use if you wanted to do these things?
  a find words to put in a poem or song   dictionary of quotations
  b understand some very informal expressions   bilingual dictionary
  c find a famous saying to include in a speech   monolingual dictionary
  d find translations of words into another language   dictionary of slang
  e read definitions of words   rhyming dictionary

go to Useful language p. 86

A Alphabetical order

1 Imagine that you want to find the information below to complete a crossword puzzle. Which books would you use to find the information? Match a–d with the book covers 1–4.

   a words that mean the same as *follower* 3
   b the meaning of *brass instrument* ☐
   c an idiom containing the word *ground* ☐
   d the first names of the actors Laurel and Hardy ☐

1 CAMBRIDGE Idioms Dictionary
2 The HUTCHINSON ENCYCLOPEDIA
3 Pocket THESAURUS
4 Cambridge Advanced Learner's Dictionary

Learning tip

We use reference books for finding specific pieces of information. Each double page of an alphabetically ordered reference book has two words in bold at the top of the pages. These show the first and last entries on those two pages. Our knowledge of the alphabet helps us to scan the reference book to find the words we are looking for.

2 You are looking for a–d in Exercise 1. Look at the words below. Underline the words which will be on the pages containing the information you want.

   a FLY – FOLD   FOLK – FOOD
   b BOXROOM – BRANCH   BRANCH LINE – BREAK
   c GREAT – GRIP   GRIPS – GUM
   d LAUD – LAUSANNE   LAVA – LAWRENCE

3 Read the reference book entries on the right and find the information in Exercise 1.

brass [MUSICAL INSTRUMENTS] /brɑːs/ *adj* [before noun] (of a musical instrument) made of metal and played by blowing: *The trumpet and trombone are brass instruments.* ○ *He plays in the brass section of the orchestra.*

Laurel and Hardy Stan Laurel (1890–1965) and Oliver Hardy (1892–1957) US film comedians. (Laurel was English-born.) Their films include many short, silent films, *Way Out West* 1937, and *A Chump at Oxford* 1940.

ground
be thin on the ground *British & Australian* if things or people are thin on the ground, there are not many of them ● *Bears are getting rather thin on the ground in European forests.* ● *I get the impression work is a bit thin on the ground at the moment.*

follower *noun* **1** disciple, adherent, partisan, pupil. **2** supporter, enthusiast, devotee, fan, servant, attendant, companion.

4 Match entries a–d below with the reference books in Exercise 1. What type of reference book is entry e from?

a
Channel Islands group of islands in the English Channel, off the northwest coast of France; they are a possession of the British crown. They comprise the islands of Jersey, Guernsey, Alderney, Great and Little Sark, with the lesser Herm, Brechou, Jethou, and Libou.

insect any of a vast group of small invertebrate animals with hard segmented bodies, three pairs of jointed legs, and, usually, two pairs of wings. On the head is a pair of feelers, or antennae. ☐Z

b
Lycra /ˈlaɪkrə/ *noun* [U] TRADEMARK a stretchy material used especially for making clothes which fit very tightly: *a Lycra swimsuit* ○ *Lycra leggings* ○ *These jeans have added Lycra for comfort and fit.*

metal E /ˈmetəl/ *noun* [C or U] a chemical element, such as iron or gold, or a mixture of such elements, such as steel, which electricity and heat can travel through and which is generally hard and strong: *Metal, paper and glass can be recycled.* ○ *Silver, gold and platinum are precious metals.* ○ *The wooden beam is reinforced with a metal plate.* ☐

c
mental

make a mental note
to make an effort to remember something, often something that you want to do later ● (often + to do sth) *I made a mental note to call my mother and tell her what he'd said.* ● (often + **that**) *Last time we had dinner together I made a mental note that you didn't like fish.* ☐

d
stare *verb* **1** gaze, gape, goggle, gawk (inf). ☐
● *noun* gaze, look, glare.

e
Lord of the Rings: The Return of the King, The
(2003 Ger/NZ/US 201m)
d Peter Jackson *p* Barrie M Osborne, Peter Jackson, Fran Walsh cast Elijah Wood, Ian McKellen, Liv Tyler, Viggo Mortensen, Sean Astin, Cate Blanchett, John Rhys-Davies, Bernard Hill, Billy Boyd, Dominic Monaghan, Orlando Bloom, Hugo Weaving, Miranda Otto, David Wenham, Andy Serkiss, Ian Holm, Sean Bean.

Focus on ...
pronunciation

Dictionaries can also help you with the pronunciation of a word. Some dictionaries, for example the *Cambridge Advanced Learner's Dictionary*, use the International Phonetic Alphabet (IPA), e.g. /brɑːs/. Look again at the reference book entries on this page and circle two more examples of phonetics.

5 Do as much of this crossword puzzle as you can. Use the reference book entries in Exercises 3 and 4 to help you with the answers.

Across
1 Hard workers are '___ on the ground'. [4]
5 *The Lord of the Rings: The Return of the* ___ [4]
7 View or belief [7]
8 ___ fabrics, like Lycra ™, are comfortable to wear. [8]
10 ___ Blanchett, *The Lord of the Rings* actress [4]
12 Air pollution, especially in cities [4]
14 Type of metal [8]
16 Choose again [8]
17 Stare [4]
18 ___ Laurel and Oliver Hardy. [4]
19 Joins [8]
22 Teach [7]
23 Soldiers are in this. [4]
24 'A friend in ___ is a friend indeed.' [4]

Down
1 You've got ten of these. [4]
2 I'll 'make a mental ___' of it. [4]
3 Follower [8]
4 Minute *adj* [4]
5 There's someone ___ at the door! [8]
6 Draughts is one. [4]
9 The ___ , the last of Shakespeare's plays [7]
11 Brass instrument [7]
13 One of the Channel Islands [8]
15 On an insect's head [8]
18 A piece of living room furniture [4]
19 Members are in this [4]
20 *East of* ____ , James Dean film (1955) [4]
21 Opposite of 'bought' [4]

6 If you haven't been able to complete the crossword, use reference books to help you find the rest of the answers. Decide what type of reference book might be useful in each case.

B It'll be in here

1 Look at this list of questions. Can you answer any of them? Which ones?

a Which word do British people use instead of the American English word *tub*? bath

b What do Americans say instead of the British English word *autumn*?

c If someone can't see very well, you can say that this person is 'as … as a … '.

d When did Emperor Hirohito of Japan die?

e You see a car with the letters *RP* next to its number plate. Where is the car from?

f When was the Golden Gate Bridge in San Francisco built?

g Who won the World Cup in 1950?

h You see this symbol *&c* in a report. What does it mean?

i Which bone is your tibia?

j A friend has written *F2F* in a text message. What does it mean?

k What is the brightest star in the galaxy?

l You see *RSVP* at the end of an invitation. What does it stand for?

2 The answers to the questions in Exercise 1 are in the *Chambers Book of Facts*. Read the introduction to the book and think about which section each answer might be in. For example, the answer to question a might be in *Nations of the World*, *Communication* or *Arts and Culture*.

CHAMBERS BOOK OF FACTS
NEW EDITION
Essential one-stop factfinder
Over 200,000 facts and figures

Chambers Book of Facts is a goldmine of valuable information for use at home, in the workplace, at school, college and university. It contains a wealth of facts and figures on a wide range of subjects, as well as many useful features including mini-biographies and up-to-date sports results.

Information is arranged into fourteen major sections, and is clearly presented with the help of diagrams, tables, lists and maps. A two-colour layout and a helpful index make essential facts easy to find.

Includes fourteen major sections:

- Space
- Earth
- Climate and Environment
- Nations of the World
- Social Structure
- History
- Time
- Natural History
- Human Body, Health and Nutrition
- Communication
- Science and Technology
- Arts and Culture
- Sports and Games
- Thought and Belief

3 Look at the headings in the *Communication* section. Check which questions in Exercise 1 you will be able to answer from this section. Match each question you can answer with a heading.

COMMUNICATION

Languages: number of speakers
Speakers of English
Foreign words and phrases
Differences between British and US
  English *question a*
Proverbs
Common abbreviations
Alphabets
British sign language: fingerspelling
US sign language: fingerspelling
Semaphore
Some common similes
-isms
Typefaces
First name meanings in the UK and USA
Forms of address
Computer languages
Emoticons
Abbreviations and acronyms used in
  e-mail
Abbreviations and acronyms used in text
  messages
News agencies
National newspapers – Europe
National newspapers – UK
Major newspapers – USA
Symbols in general use
Clothes care symbols
Road signs
Car index marks – UK
Car index marks – international
UK airports
International airports
Airline designators
Air distances
Flying times
European road distances
UK road distances
International E-road network
  ('Euroroutes')
Deepwater ports of the world
Map of Europe

Did you know …?

A *simile* is a phrase which compares one thing to something else, using the words *like* or *as*, for example 'as white as snow'. A *proverb* is a famous phrase or sentence which gives you advice. 'You can't judge a book by its cover', for example, means that appearances can be deceptive.

4 Read some of the entries in the *Communication* section and find the answers to as many questions in Exercise 1 as possible.

Differences between British and US English

British	US
aeroplane	airplane
aluminium	aluminum
anticlockwise	counterclockwise
aubergine	eggplant
autumn	fall
back garden	yard
banknote	bill
bath	tub
biscuit (savoury)	cracker
biscuit (sweet)	cookie

Some common similes

as bald as a coot
as black as ink or pitch
as blind as a bat
as blue as the sky
as bold as brass
as bright as a button
as brown as a berry
as calm as a millpond
as clean as a whistle
as clear as a bell or as crystal
  or (*ironically*) as mud

Abbreviations and acronyms used in text messages

B	Be
BCNU	Be seeing you
BFN	Bye for now
B4	Before
C	See
CD	Could
COZ	Because
CU	See you
DA	The
EVRY1	Everyone
EZ	Easy
4EVER	Forever
F2F	Face to face
FWD	Forward

Common abbreviations

RPI	retail price index
RPM	resale price maintenance
rpm	revolutions per minute
RRP	recommended retail price
RS	Royal Society
RSI	repetitive strain injury
RSPB	Royal Society for the Protection of Birds
RSPCA	Royal Society for the Prevention of Cruelty to Animals
RSVP	répondez s'il vous plaît (please reply)
RTG	radio-isotope thermoelectric generator

Symbols in general use

&	ampersand
&c	et cetera
@	at; per (in costs)
×	by (measuring dimensions. eg 3 x 4)
£	pound
$	dollar (also peso, escudo, etc in certain countries)
¢	cent (also centavo, etc in certain countries)
©	copyright
®	registered trademark
¶	new paragraph

Car index marks – international

RIM	Mauritania
RL	Lebanon
RM	Madagascar
RMM	Mali
RN	Niger
RO	Romania
ROK	Korea, Republic of
ROU	Uruguay
RP	Philippines
RSM	San Marino

5 Have you learned anything else while you have been looking for the answers to the questions?

E Xtra practice

Look for the answers to any unanswered questions either in a book of facts or on the Internet. Try the online encyclopaedia www.wikipedia.org

Class bonus

Write some general knowledge questions about different topics. The website www.soyouthinkyouknowitall.com contains questions you could use. Click on Play more quizzes and browse the topic list. Exchange your questions with a partner. Can you find the answers to your partner's questions before the next lesson?

Can-do checklist

Tick what you can do.

	Can do	Need more practice
I can find information in a reference book.	✓	✓
I can use reference books to complete a crossword.		
I can find answers to questions in a reference book.		

Get ready to **read**

○ Read this dictionary definition of *fiction*.
Some people enjoy reading fiction more than non-fiction.
Which do you prefer? Why?

> **fiction** /ˈfɪkʃ°n/ *noun* **1** [U] literature and stories about imaginary people or events *What's the best-selling children's fiction title?* ➔Opposite **non-fiction. 2** [U, no plural] something that is not true or real ➔See also: **science fiction.**

○ Which of these types of fiction and non-fiction do you enjoy?
Tick ✓ the types you like.

science fiction ☐   biographies ☐   detective stories ☐   romantic novels ☐
cookery books ☐   horror stories ☐   travel books ☐   health and fitness books ☐

○ Read the questions and underline the answer that is the most true for you.
How often do you use your college or university library?   *every day / once a week / once a month / never*
How often do you use a public library?   *every day / once a week / once a month / never*
Which of these have you recently borrowed from a library?   *a textbook for study / a novel / a CD / a DVD*

go to Useful language p. 86

A Using a library catalogue

1 Imagine you live in Oxfordshire, UK and you want to find out how to use the catalogue for your local libraries. Which of these things do you think the catalogue does? Tick ✓ one or more of the boxes.

a lists all the books that the libraries in the area hold ☐
b provides biographical information about the author of each book ☐
c shows which library has each book ☐
d tells you what's on the shelves and what's on loan ☐
e gives readers' recommendations for each book ☐

2 Scan the webpage on the right from the Oxfordshire County Council website and check your answers to Exercise 1. What else does the catalogue do?

----

3 Scan the webpage again and answer these questions.

a How many ways can you search the catalogue? ......
b How many matching titles can be shown on the first page? ......
c How many matching titles can be shown in total? ......
d How many types of catalogue can you search? ......

---

http://www.libcat.oxfordshire.gov.uk/

Oxfordshire County Council – Library Catalogue
www.oxfordshire.gov.uk

Library Catalogue Help

Introduction

• The catalogue gives you details of all the titles in stock, including books, DVDs, videos, audio books, language courses, printed music, recorded music, etc. It tells you in which libraries the titles are held and whether they are currently available for you to reserve or borrow.

Searching the Catalogue

• You can search the catalogue by keyword, author, title, author/keyword, class number, series or ISBN.
• To enter text into a search box, you must first select the box by clicking the left mouse button on it. Once you have entered the words, click on the search button or press the Return key to begin your search.

Search Results

• Search results displays a list of titles that match your search criteria. The first ten titles will be shown and you can click on the button at the bottom of the page to see more items, if available. You can adjust the number of titles displayed per page by clicking on the down arrow in the box at the top of the list. Each catalogue search will return a list containing a maximum of 100 matching items.
• You can limit your search to specific areas of the catalogue by using the three Options buttons (Whole catalogue, Book catalogue or Sound and vision catalogue).

4 Read the webpage on the right about Keyword Search. What can you use this search for? Tick ✓ one of the boxes.

a to find a specific book ☐
b to find all the books on a specific topic ☐
c both of the above ☐

5 Should you do the following when you do a Keyword Search? Write **Y** (yes) or **N** (no) after each statement.

a You should be as exact as possible when you choose your keyword(s). _Y_
b You should try to use five keywords. ......
c You should put a space between keywords. ......
d You should put the subject name first and then the author's name. ......

6 One of your searches gives you very few results. What could you do to get more?

Did you know …?

The Dewey Decimal System of Classification is used in the UK and the USA to organize library collections. It groups together materials on the same subject by using a special numbering system. It consists of ten general classes, which are then further subdivided. For example, 400 is Language, and 423 is English dictionaries. The system was invented by an American librarian, Melvil Dewey, in the 1870s.

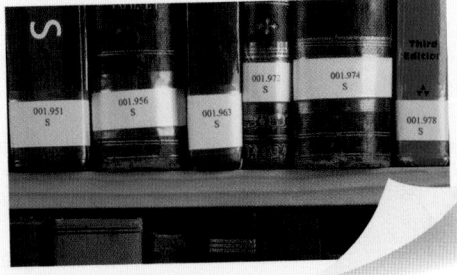

E☒tra practice

Find out if your library uses the Dewey Decimal System of Classification. Use the catalogue to find books on 'reading skills'.

Keyword Search

- Searching by keyword is a powerful and effective way of finding the information you want from the catalogue.
- The keyword search will work on any combination of words from author, title, series or subject in any order. You can also use the keyword search if you can only partly remember details of an item. For example, to find a book on India written by Dervla Murphy, enter INDIA MURPHY.
- Enter as many keywords as required, separating each keyword with a space. The maximum number of keywords is four.
- You can use the keyword search if you are looking for a particular subject, for example ACID RAIN, STONEHENGE, or CAKE DECORATING.
- Try to make your choice of words as specific as possible. For example, look for STEAM TRAINS not RAILWAYS, or, if looking for a book on roses, use the word ROSE, rather than GARDENING. This will return a smaller list which will meet your requirements more precisely.
- However, if you only type in one word (especially if it is a common one) you may get a long and not very helpful list of matches. On the other hand, too many keywords may narrow your search too far; don't be afraid to experiment!

7 You want to find items a–f in the library catalogue. Write suitable keywords for each item.

a a book by somebody Paton with *cry* and *country* in the title
   Paton cry country

b a biography of the Brazilian footballer Ronaldinho
----

c *The Remains of the Day* – you don't know the author's name
----

d some information about how to play backgammon
----

e a book about the history of classical music by Howard Goodall
----

f a book to help you improve your reading skills
----

8 Read the webpage below about Class Search. Imagine you want to find the classification number for 'English'. How many ways of finding it does the webpage mention? Underline them.

Class Search

- The library stock is classified according to the Dewey Decimal system, where a number corresponds to a particular subject. If you know the number associated with the subject in which you are interested, you can search for all books with that classification number. This is a good way to search for books on your chosen topic if you know the number. Library staff can help you find the right number, or, if you know of another book on the same subject, you can see what class number it has been given, and use that number in your search. For example: type the class number 001.6 for books about computing, or type 001 for all class numbers starting with 001. Then press the Return key.

9 You are at a library in Oxfordshire. What kind of books would you look for in the catalogue?

B 4.50 from Paddington

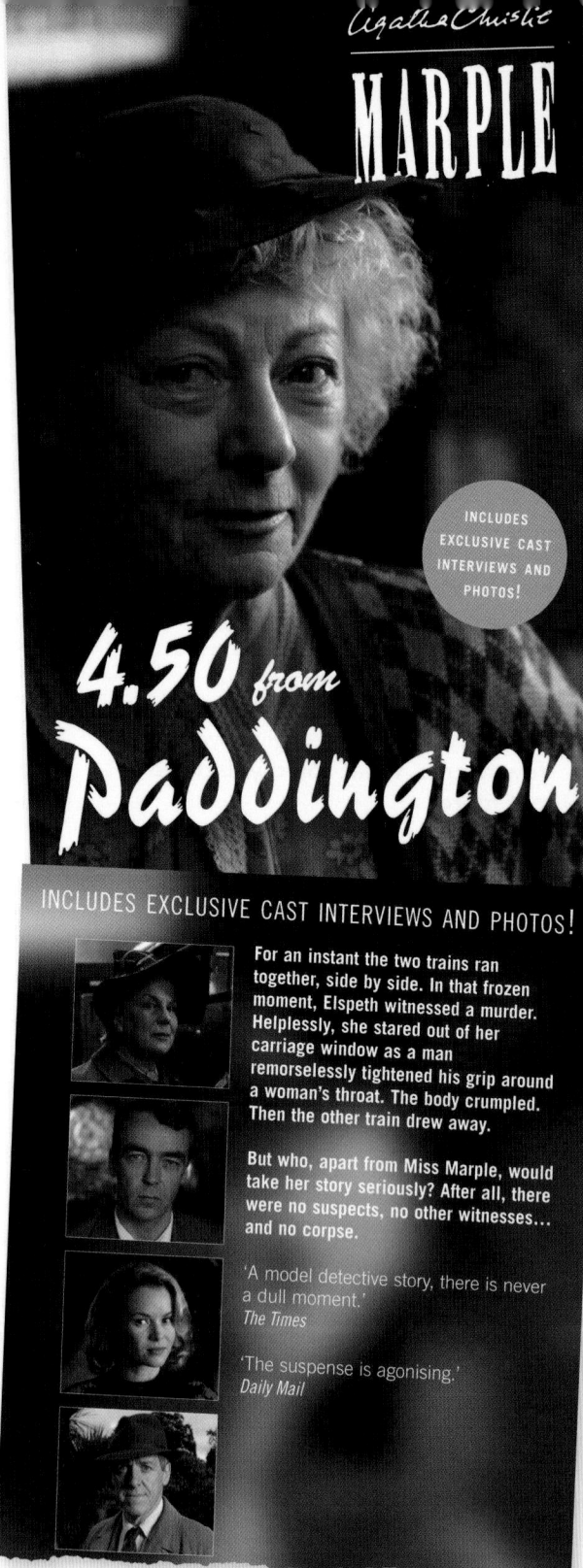

Learning tip

Reading whole articles, stories and books is a good way to improve your extensive reading skills so that reading for study becomes easier.

When you go to a bookshop or library, choose books that you are interested in. Skim two or three pages and make sure there are not too many new words (a maximum of ten per page). If there are more, you won't be able to work out their meaning from the other words in the text. Direct speech breaks up the text and is generally easier than narrative or descriptive writing.

When you start reading, don't stop in the middle of a sentence or paragraph and go back – continue until the end of a page or chapter.

1 **Look at the front and back cover of this book and read the blurb (the description of the book). Then answer the questions.**

a Who is the book by? _____

b What is it about? _____

c Is there a film version of this book?

_____

2 **What do you know about the author? Have you read any of her books in your own language? Guess the missing numbers in these sentences.**

a She wrote _____ crime novels and _____ plays.

b Her books have been translated into _____ languages.

c More than _____ of her books have been sold in total.

3 **Now read part of the introduction to the book and check your answers to Exercise 2.**

Agatha Christie is known throughout the world as the Queen of Crime. Her books have sold over a billion copies in English with another billion in 100 foreign languages. She is the most widely published author of all time and in any language, outsold only by the Bible and Shakespeare. She is the author of 80 crime novels and short story collections, 19 plays, and six novels written under the name of Mary Westmacott.

4 **Read the extract from the book on the opposite page. Do you think this extract is from near the beginning or near the end of the story?**

_____

For an instant the two trains ran together, side by side. In that frozen moment, Elspeth witnessed a murder. Helplessly, she stared out of her carriage window as a man remorselessly tightened his grip around a woman's throat. The body crumpled. Then the other train drew away.

But who, apart from Miss Marple, would take her story seriously? After all, there were no suspects, no other witnesses... and no corpse.

'A model detective story, there is never a dull moment.'
The Times

'The suspense is agonising.'
Daily Mail

5 **The name 'Mrs McGillicuddy' isn't on the back cover of the book. Look at the back cover again and circle Mrs McGillicuddy's first name.**

6 **Does the ticket collector think Mrs McGillicuddy is telling the truth? Underline the parts of the text that help you decide.**

The door of her compartment was drawn back and a ticket collector said, 'Ticket, please'.

Mrs McGillicuddy turned to him with vehemence.

'A woman has been strangled,' she said. 'In a train that has just passed. I saw it.'

The ticket collector looked at her doubtfully.

'I beg your pardon, madam?'

'A man strangled a woman! In a train. I saw it – through there.' She pointed to the window.

The ticket collector looked extremely doubtful.

'Strangled?' he said disbelievingly.

'Yes, *strangled*! I saw it, I tell you. You must *do* something at once!'

The ticket collector coughed apologetically.

'You don't think, madam, that you may had a little nap and – er –' he broke off tactfully.

'I have had a nap, but if you think this was a dream, you're quite wrong. I *saw* it, I tell you.'

The ticket collector's eyes dropped to the open magazine lying on the seat. On the exposed page was a girl being strangled whilst a man with a revolver threatened the pair from an open doorway.

He said persuasively: 'Now don't you think, madam, that you'd been reading an exciting story, and that you just dropped off, and awaking a little confused –'

Mrs McGillicuddy interrupted him.

'I *saw* it,' she said. 'I was as wide awake as you are. And I looked out of the window into the window of the train alongside, and a man was strangling a woman. And what I want to know is, what are you going to do about it?'

'Well – madam –'

'You're going to do *something*, I suppose?'

The ticket collector sighed reluctantly and glanced at his watch.

'We shall be in Brackhampton in exactly seven minutes. I'll report what you've told me. In what direction was the train you mention going?'

'This direction, of course. You don't suppose I'd have been able to see this if a train had flashed past going in the other direction?'

The ticket collector looked as though he thought Mrs McGillicuddy was quite capable of seeing anything anywhere as the fancy took her. But he remained polite.

'You can rely on me, madam,' he said. 'I will report your statement. Perhaps I might have your name and address – just in case …'

7 Do you think you might be interested in reading this book? Why? / Why not?

Focus on …
adverbs

Find the words *doubtfully* and *disbelievingly* in the extract and complete these sentences.

a The _____ doubtfully.

b _____ disbelievingly.

These words are adverbs and they describe how someone – in this case, the ticket collector – did something.

Find four more adverbs that describe the ticket collector's actions. What did he do, and how did he do it? Write the verb and the adverb.

c The ticket collector _____

d he _____

e He _____

f The ticket collector _____

Complete these sentences with the six adverbs from sentences a–f.

g 'Is he really an astronaut?' she asked
    _____disbelievingly_____ .

h The waitress smiled _____ as she said that there was no soup.

i I didn't want to stay late and do the extra work, but in the end I agreed _____ .

j John told us his views and he spoke very
    _____ .

k 'I think you might look better in the blue sweater,' she suggested _____ .

l 'I might be able to help you tomorrow, but I'm not sure,' he said _____ .

Class bonus

Work with a partner. One of you is the ticket collector and the other is Mrs McGillicuddy. Read aloud your conversation. (Don't read out the narrative. Only read the direct speech.)

Can-do checklist

Tick what you can do.

	Can do	Need more practice
I can understand instructions in a library catalogue.		
I can understand what a novel is about from the blurb.		
I can read fiction without worrying about difficult language.		

read

- Answer these questions.
  What kinds of things have you read today? _____
  How many languages do you read regularly? _____
  What kinds of things do you read in English? _____
  What sort of difficulties do you have when you read in English? _____

- Think about these questions.

  | How important is reading in our everyday lives? | What kinds of reading do we do? | How do we read? |

- In this unit, you are going to read extracts from the entry for *Reading* in an encyclopaedia. This entry describes reading in your first language. Do you think the extracts will help you to answer the questions above?

go to Useful language p. 86

A Kinds of reading

1 Look at the statements below about reading. Do you agree with them? Tick ✓ the boxes.

		I agree.	I disagree.	I don't know.
a	Reading is the act of getting meaning from printed or written words.			
b	People may read hundreds or thousands of words a day without even looking at a book, newspaper or magazine.			
c	In the simplest sense, reading means recognizing letters and groups of letters as symbols that stand for particular sounds.			
d	In most cases, the teaching of reading stresses certain skills, such as word recognition, vocabulary development, and comprehension (understanding of reading matter).			

2 The statements in Exercise 1 are the first sentences of the first four paragraphs of the encyclopaedia entry for *Reading*. Here is the rest of one of the paragraphs. Which paragraph (a–d) is it from?

It is basic to learning and one of the most important skills in everyday life. Reading provides the key to all kinds of information. It enables us to learn how to build or fix things, to enjoy stories, to discover what other people believe, and to develop ideas and beliefs of our own.

Learning tip

When we read a long text for the first time, we usually skim it in order to find out the general meaning and to identify the parts which we want to read in detail. The most important parts of the text are the first paragraph, which introduces the overall topic, and the first sentence of each of the other paragraphs. This sentence usually introduces the topic of the paragraph.

3 Read the extract from the entry on the right and <u>underline</u> the most important points.

4 Are any of the ideas in the extract new to you? Which ones?

5 Which of the three reading styles – recreational, study-type, survey – have you used to read this extract?

6 Read the extract again. (Circle) the correct phrases so that the sentences are true.

  a Older readers often understand a text more easily because they know more *about reading techniques /* (*information*) than younger readers.

  b Good readers use different reading techniques for different *subjects / types of text*.

  c Often when we reread part of a story we do this because we *like / can't believe* it.

  d When we do study-type reading, we try to *find just the main ideas / link the main ideas together*.

  e With survey reading, we read *everything / only some parts* carefully.

  f Beginners find reading easier if the text uses language that *they know / is new*.

7 Does the text describe your experiences as a reader of your own language and of other languages?

Kinds of reading

People differ in reading ability. For example, those who have been reading a long time tend to understand what they have read more quickly and more automatically than do new readers. In addition, older readers bring more background experiences to their reading. They can use their experiences to fill in important information that is not clearly stated in the text.

A good reader uses various reading techniques. The technique depends on the type and difficulty of the material, the purpose for reading it, and the reader's own language development and familiarity with the subject.

Reading can be classified into three main kinds: (1) recreational reading, (2) study-type reading, and (3) survey reading. Good readers can easily shift from one kind to another, depending on their purpose for reading and on the material itself.

Recreational reading can provide hour after hour of enjoyment. When reading a story purely for pleasure, most people read at a relaxed, uneven speed. They may skim through a tale until they come to a scene, a description, or even a phrase that is especially pleasing or satisfying. That portion may be read slowly and then reread to be enjoyed, appreciated, or considered.

Study-type reading usually requires the reader to pay close attention to the text. A good reader looks for significant ideas and details. The reader then tries to understand how those ideas and details relate to one another and how they fit into the general topic. Reading speed tends to be slower the first time study-type material is read, and the reader may need to reread portions of the text to understand it fully. Reading speed may be much faster when the material is reviewed.

Survey reading involves covering a large amount of text to get a general idea of its content. In such cases, the person may first skim the material to understand the main point. The reader may then look for details that reinforce or illustrate that point. The person may then read some sections carefully to make sure that the desired information has been found.

Shifting among kinds of reading. Most people use different reading techniques for different reading situations. For example, a mystery enjoyed simply for entertainment may be read rapidly. But a classic Russian novel may call for slow, careful reading. Technical texts that could lead to job advancement or that tell how to fix something usually require thoughtful reading.

Good readers can easily shift from one kind of reading to another. For instance, a student collecting information to write a paper might begin surveying articles to see if they fit the topic. One article may lead the student to consider changing the topic, and so the article is studied thoroughly and another topic chosen. While surveying for the new topic, the student looks for information to create an outline. During the survey reading, the student may see an entertaining article and read it for pleasure.

Reading flexibility improves with experience. Beginners may tend to read everything somewhat awkwardly, advancing slowly word by word because they doubt their ability to recognize words. By reading materials that follow their own language patterns – that is, familiar words and sentences they use – even beginning readers can read with both speed and understanding. In time, they learn that different reading materials make different demands on their abilities.

8 What advice would you give to someone who wanted to improve their reading?

E X tra practice

Look at the texts you have already read in this book. Decide which reading styles you used with each one.

B How we read

1 Read another extract from the encyclopaedia entry for *Reading*. This extract deals with these three topics. Put them in the order in which they appear in the text.

a the importance of memory in reading ☐

b the physical process of reading ☐

c how to deal with unfamiliar words ☐

2 Think about the topics in Exercise 1. Skim the extract and decide which paragraphs you need to read more carefully to find out about each topic.

Topic a _____

Topic b _____

Topic c _____

3 Read the paragraphs about the physical process of reading. As you read, think about the words in *italics*. Why are they in *italics*? Tick ✓ one of the boxes.

a They are technical terms that are probably unfamiliar to most readers. ☐

b They are important and difficult words that the reader has to understand. ☐

c They are words that are explained in the paragraph. ☐

d More than one of the above. ☐

e All of the above. ☐

Did you know …?

Italic type takes its name from Italy. It is characteristic of the typefaces used by early Italian printers, such as the Aldine Press of Venice. Originally italic type was used for entire texts; it was first used as a secondary typeface in the 18th century.

How we read

[1] Reading depends first on our *perceiving* (seeing and recognizing) written or printed letters and words. We must then be able to comprehend what we perceive.

[2] **Perceiving reading matter.** The process of reading begins as our eyes see *visual stimuli* – that is, the printed or written symbols that make up what is to be read. Eye movements across the symbols capture the stimuli. Eye movements called *saccadic movements* take place as our eyes move across a page, pausing briefly to take in groups of words. As our eyes move across a line, they alternatively pause and move on. The pauses are called *fixations*. Another type of eye movement, *regression*, occurs when our eyes shift back to reread a word or group of words. To move from one line to the next, our eyes use a movement called a *return sweep*. However, good readers are unaware of their eye movements as they read.

[3] **Comprehending what is perceived.** Reading involves far more than simply seeing visual stimuli. You must first choose a particular piece to satisfy some purpose. That purpose not only determines the selection of the text but also helps you decide which experiences and reading skills to use to comprehend the material. Your purpose may also suggest how you might use any new knowledge or understanding that you gain from the material.

[4] While reading, you draw on numerous ideas and feelings stored in your memory. Those ideas and feelings make up your *background*. You also rely on verbal memory – that is, an understanding of how words come together and form more complex ideas.

[5] Your background and verbal memory change and grow with each reading experience. Information in new material blends with your past experiences and may correct misunderstandings, provide fresh knowledge, broaden interests, or help solve problems.

[6] In many cases, readers lack the background and verbal memory needed to comprehend a text quickly and easily. Such readers may use techniques called *word-recognition strategies*. The more experienced a reader becomes, the more automatically the reader applies these strategies to comprehend unfamiliar words.

[7] Readers can use several general types of word-recognition strategies. For example, a reader who does not know the meaning of a particular word may look for *context clues* in the surrounding text. These clues may be either *semantic* or *syntactic*. When using semantic clues, the reader tries to relate the word to other information or illustrations in the material. Semantic clues include comparisons and contrasts, definitions, descriptions, and the placement of new words near familiar words that help explain their meaning. A reader may also rely on syntactic clues – that is, the word's position and grammatical use in the text. For example, deciding whether a word is functioning as a noun, verb, adjective, or adverb can help a reader figure out its meaning.

[8] In a word-recognition strategy called *structural analysis*, a reader uses clues within the word itself to guess what the word means. The reader relies on knowledge of the meanings of prefixes, suffixes, *roots* (word bases), compound words, and endings such as *ed* and *ing*, and of how they are combined. For example, the adverb *undoubtedly* has the prefix *un*, the root *doubt*, ending *ed*, and the suffix *ly*. Knowing the meanings of the parts of the word leads the reader to decide that the word means *without doubt*. And without doubt the best way for readers to add such knowledge to verbal memory is to encounter words made of those parts in text they find meaningful, and to use the words in conversation and writing.

Class bonus

Choose either the topic of 'the importance of memory' or 'how to deal with unfamiliar words'. Work with someone who has chosen the same topic and read the paragraphs about it again. Help each other with any difficulties in the text.

4 Read about topics a and c from Exercise 1 – the importance of memory in reading, and how to deal with unfamiliar words. Are these sentences true (T) or false (F)?

a Our verbal memory only helps us to understand verbs. __F__

b You can improve your background and verbal memory by reading more. ......

c Good readers don't need to use word-recognition strategies. ......

d Other words in the text can help us understand an unfamiliar word. ......

e Structural analysis is a way of examining the different parts of a word to understand its meaning. ......

5 Which of the three word-recognition strategies – semantic context clues, syntactic context clues, structural analysis – have you used to read this text?

6 Think of a time when you had difficulty reading something in English or in your own language. Why was it difficult? Did you lack the background or the verbal memory?

7 What advice would you give to someone who wanted to improve their reading?

Focus on ...
prefixes and suffixes

Prefixes and suffixes are groups of letters which are added to words to make new words. In this extract, the verb *read* appears with the prefix *re* (*reread*) and the suffix *ing* (*reading*). A prefix has its own meaning, which becomes part of the meaning of the new word.

A suffix can change the word class of a word, e.g. *comfort* (noun), *comfortable* (adjective), make a word plural (*word*, *words*), or change the tense of a verb (*need*, *needed*).

Add prefixes or suffixes to make words in the extract.

a ....move _ments_ .. (paragraph 2)

b ....aware.......... (paragraph 2)

c ....select.......... (paragraph 3)

d ....inform.......... (paragraph 5)

e ....understand.......... (paragraph 5)

f ....know.......... (paragraph 5)

Now complete these sentences. Use the words in a–f above but with different prefixes or suffixes. You might need to use your dictionary.

g It is impossible to remain ..... _unmoved_ ..... by some of the awful stories in the news.

h Environmental .... has increased dramatically over the past decade.

i He's very .... about the people he spends time with.

j It is believed that an .... has given the police the names of three of the gang.

k It's .... that he's angry – his car was badly damaged.

l Ask Ahmed about the Pyramids. He's very .... about Egyptian history.

Can-do checklist

Tick what you can do.

	Can do	Need more practice
I can skim a text and identify the main points.		
I can identify the topic of each paragraph within a text.		
I can relate what I have read to my own experiences.		

A Are these statements true (T) or false (F)?

1 You can often use other words in the text to work out the meaning of an unknown word. ...... (Unit 9)
2 If an email is sent to someone else and you are copied in, you don't need to read the email. ...... (Unit 10)
3 Writers use linking words and expressions to show the relationships between different ideas in a text. ...... (Unit 11)
4 Formal letters may contain language which we don't use in our everyday lives. ...... (Unit 12)
5 Charts and graphs can present figures more directly than a piece of text. ...... (Unit 13)
6 We skim reference books in order to find what we are looking for. ...... (Unit 14)
7 It is easier to work out the meaning of unknown words from context if there are not too many of them on the page. ...... (Unit 15)
8 Reading the first sentence of each paragraph will not help you to get a general idea of what the text is about. ...... (Unit 16)

B Now read the *Learning tips* for Units 9–16 on pages 89–91. Do you want to change any of your answers in Exercise A?

C Skim Texts A–D on the opposite page. What is each text, or where does it come from? Use the words in the list.

| an email a leaflet a letter a novel a questionnaire |
| a non-fiction book a report a webpage |

9 Text A ....
10 Text B ....
11 Text C ....
12 Text D ....

D Read Text A and find the following words. Match the words with descriptions a–c. Write the letters in the boxes.

13 blog ☐   16 email ☐
14 computer ☐   17 virus ☐
15 hardware ☐

a a new word
b a word whose original meaning is still in use and which also has a new meaning
c a word whose original meaning is no longer in use, but which now has a new meaning

E Read Text B. Which of this information does Linda provide? (✓ = information given, ✗ = information not given)

18 the taxi company that Sofia should contact ☐
19 where Linda is flying to ☐
20 when the taxi should pick her up ☐
21 where it should pick her up from ☐
22 when she is coming back ☐

F Read Text C. Choose the five adjectives which best describe Linnet Ridgeway. Write the letters in the boxes in alphabetical order.

23 ☐   24 ☐   25 ☐   26 ☐   27 ☐

a blonde
b confident
c elderly
d elegant
e famous
f friendly
g good-looking
h intelligent
i rich
j shy

G Look at the tables in Text D. They show the top six exporters and importers of watches and clocks between 2002 and 2005. Circle the correct words in the sentences.

28 The value of Switzerland's exports rose by the greatest amount in *2003 / 2004 / 2005*.
29 The total value of Germany's exports was *the same as / less than / more than* the total value of its imports during this four-year period.
30 The value of Hong Kong's exports rose *by the same amount as / less than / more than* the value of its imports in this period.
31 Italy was the fifth highest importer in *one / two / three* of the years.
32 From its position in exports in 2004, Japan *rose a position / dropped a position / stayed in the same position* in 2005.

Text A

Wanted: A computer, female aged 18–25

Over the last 30 years, the biggest source of neologisms or new words in English has probably been computing. *Internet* first appeared in 1986, for instance, and has since become an everyday word for many people. *Email* first appeared in 1982 and *blog* in 1998.

New ideas are not only expressed by coining words. Even more common is adding fresh meanings to existing words. Still within the computing field, the words *mouse*, *hardware*, *program*, *virus* and *monitor* have all taken on new meanings in the last 50 years, but they continue to be used with their original senses – a mouse is still a small rodent as well as a computing device.

When a new meaning is added, however, the original sense is not always retained. A *computer* used to be a role involving lots of addition and subtraction. With the introduction of calculators and machine computers, there was no longer any need for human computers, and the job-related meaning of the word became obsolete. Nowadays, a 1930s recruitment advert such as the one in the title of this chapter sounds very strange.

Text B

Delete Reply Reply All Forward Print

Hi Sofia
Do you think you could book me a taxi for Monday morning? My flight leaves at 9.40 am, so I'd better be at the airport at 7.40 at the latest. Can you ask the taxi company to confirm what time they'll pick me up (they should know how long it'll take at that time of day from Debden to Luton Airport). My address is Raymond's Cottage (it's the white house on the main street opposite the newsagent's) and the phone number is (01779) 54481. Thanks!
Linda

PS I won't need a return taxi. My husband's going to pick me up on Friday evening.

Text C

LINNET RIDGEWAY!

"That's *Her*!" said Mr. Burnaby, the landlord of the Three Crowns.

He nudged his companion.

The two men stared with round bucolic eyes and slightly open mouths.

A big scarlet Rolls Royce had just stopped in front of the local post office.

A girl jumped out, a girl without a hat and wearing a frock that looked (but only looked) simple. A girl with golden hair and straight autocratic features – a girl with a lovely shape – a girl such as was seldom seen in Malton-under-Wode.

With a quick imperative step she passed into the post office.

"That's her!" said Mr. Burnaby again. And he went on in a low awed voice. "Millions she's got. ... Going to spend thousands on the place. Swimming pools there's going to be, and Italian gardens and a ballroom and half of the house pulled down and rebuilt ..."

"She'll bring money into the town," said his friend.

He was a lean, seedy-looking man. His tone was envious and grudging.

Mr. Burnaby agreed.

"Yes, it's a great thing for Malton-under-Wode. A great thing it is."

Text D

Watches and clocks: exports 2002–2005 (US$ bn)

	2002	2003	2004	2005
Switzerland	6.8	7.6	8.9	9.9
Hong Kong*	4.9	5.4	5.9	5.9
China	1.7	1.9	2.1	2.0
Germany	0.7	0.9	1.0	1.1
Japan	1.0	1.0	1.1	0.9
France	0.6	0.7	0.7	0.8

Watches and clocks: imports 2002–2005 (US$ bn)

	2002	2003	2004	2005
Hong Kong*	3.8	4.1	4.6	4.7
United States	3.3	3.7	3.9	4.0
Japan	1.7	1.8	2.1	2.2
Italy	0.9	1.0	1.2	1.2
Switzerland	1.0	1.0	1.2	1.2
Germany	0.9	1.1	1.2	1.2

*Hong Kong Special Administrative Region of China

H Skim this text from a Health and Safety leaflet.

33 Who is the text for? Tick ✓ one of the boxes.
a people who work in hospitals ☐
b people who work in shops ☐
c people who work in schools ☐

34 What dangers does the text mention? Tick ✓ one of the boxes.
a dangers inside a building ☐
b dangers outside a building ☐
c dangers both inside and outside a building ☐

Slips, trips and falls are a danger to you and your customers

Pay special attention to these trouble spots

Floors

- Watch out for loose carpeting, floorboards and tiles.
- Also watch out for cracked, loose or crumbling surfaces.
- Keep the floor clear. Any small thing, even a pen, can cause a fall.

Damaged areas should be reported to your manager as soon as possible.

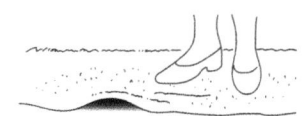

Stairs, aisles and walkways

Don't store materials on the stairs or in passageways. Keep passageways free of boxes, rubbish bins and other obstacles. (If an object is in the way, move it or walk around it. Avoid climbing over it.)

Hidden steps

When turning a corner or stepping outside, look out for steps that may not be obvious. Make sure others are aware of any hidden steps.

Spills and other wet areas

It only takes a small puddle for a serious accident to happen. Clean up spills and moisture from rain, snow or other substances immediately and place a sign to warn others of the danger.

Other slip, trip and fall hazards

Electrical leads

Don't run leads across aisles or under carpets. (This is both a fire and tripping hazard.) And don't use adaptors. If extension leads must be used, make sure they are close to the wall, where people cannot walk or trip over them.

Icy spots

Walk slowly on any icy surface. Inform your manager of any outside areas where sand or grit is needed.

Lighting

Make sure customers and colleagues can see where they're going. Report faulty lighting promptly. Use the emergency lighting where necessary and ensure it is in working order by regular testing.

General tips for preventing falls

- Be alert. Watch where you are going and what you're doing. Watch out for hazards that others might miss.
- Place warning signs or barriers around areas that may be slippery or otherwise dangerous.
- Whether you're working at heights or on the ground, be sure to follow all safety rules. Only use equipment that you've been trained and authorised to use.
- Don't take chances. Avoid tasks that are beyond your ability.

I Find the following words in the text and complete the exercise.

35 *floors*
Find three words for different types of floor surface.

---

36 *damaged areas*
Find three adjectives which describe how floors can be damaged.

---

37 *obstacle*
Write a definition of this word using other words from the paragraph.

---

38 *obstacles*
Find two examples of obstacles.

---

39 *hidden steps*
Find a word with the opposite meaning of *hidden*.

---

40 *wet areas*
Find three words for types of wet area.

---

41 *electrical lead*
Find another example of an electrical item.

---

42 *faulty lighting*
Find a phrase with the opposite meaning of *faulty*.

J Complete these sentences with an example from the text.

43 You might slip _____

44 You might trip _____

45 You might fall _____

K Kasia works in a shop. The other day she slipped and fell at work. Now she is now looking on her union's website for the answers to some questions. Read the webpage on the right and circle the answers to her questions.

46 Should there be a qualified first-aid person in all shops and offices?
yes   no

47 Should the person who looks after the first aid box be a qualified first-aider?
yes   no

48 Do I have to report my accident in the accident book?
yes   no

49 Can my boss write a different account of the accident?
yes   no

L Find verbs in the Answers on the webpage which mean the following.

50 says _____

51 make sure _____

52 officially choose (someone) _____

53 write down for the future _____

54 experience or have _____

55 tell _____

? Question

Should first aid be provided in my workplace?

Short Answer

Yes, it should. Your employer has to provide adequate first aid for their staff.

Long Answer

Regulation 3 of the Health and Safety (First Aid) Regulations 1981 states: 'An employer shall provide, or ensure that there are provided, such equipment and facilities as are adequate and appropriate in the circumstances for enabling first aid to be rendered to his employees if they are injured or become ill at work.

The level of provision will depend on the level of risk and the numbers of employees in the workplace. Guidance states that low risk workplaces like shops or offices should have qualified first-aiders when the number of staff is greater than 50. Otherwise there should be an "appointed person" who has responsibility for keeping the first aid box and calling an ambulance if it is needed. Download our Guide to First Aid for more information.

? Question

Can my employer stop me putting entries into the accident book?

Short Answer

No, they can't. The accident book is there for anyone to make an entry. They can nominate someone to do it for you, but that person must write down what you say.

Long Answer

The Social Security Regulations 1979 requires that injuries and diseases are reported and that is why there is an Accident book or a similar means of reporting. An employer might get someone to do this on your behalf for the sake of consistency, but they must record exactly what you say to them. If the employer does not agree with your version of the facts, then he can enter that in the relevant section of the report. If you encounter any problems, then you should inform your safety rep immediately.

Appendix 1
Useful language

This section contains a list of words which are important for carrying out the reading exercises for each unit. You can use the list in three ways.

1 You can look at the list before you begin the unit and make sure that you understand the meaning of the words by looking them up in a dictionary.
2 You can look at the list before you begin the unit, but try and work out the meaning of the words when you meet them in the unit.
3 You can look at the list when you have completed the unit and check that you understand the words.

When you start using the book, you may prefer to use the list in the first way. However, you will find each word in one of the texts, and the context – the words around the unknown word – will help you to work out its meaning. As you develop your reading skills, you will probably realize that it is not necessary to look at the list before you begin the unit. You may already know some of the words; you will be able to work out others from the text or the task.

Each list is a record of the vocabulary of the unit. You can use it as a checklist when you have completed the unit. There is space after each word to write a translation in your own language or an English expression using the word. Mark each word that you understand and can use with a highlighter pen.

There is also space below the wordlist for you to write other words from the unit which are important to you. Look at *Appendix 3* for ideas on what to record for each word.

Unit 1
Reading A
aubergine *noun* _____
garlic *noun* _____
(green) pepper *noun* _____
olive *noun* _____
basil *noun* _____
pine nut *noun* _____
cocoa powder *noun* _____
_____
_____
_____

Reading B
peppercorn *noun* _____
coffee bean *noun* _____
coffee filter *noun* _____
_____
_____
_____

Unit 2
Reading A
voucher *noun* _____
remark *noun* _____
terms and conditions *noun* _____
available *adjective* _____
fee *noun* _____
(bodily) injury *noun* _____
coverage *noun* _____
in effect *expression* _____
surcharge *noun* _____
waiver *noun* _____
collision *noun* _____
specified (amount) *adjective* _____
theft *noun* _____
_____
_____
_____

Reading B
in compliance with *expression* _____
in accordance with *expression* _____
_____
_____
_____

Unit**3**

Reading A
let *verb* ....
excluding *preposition* ....
professional *adjective* ....
furnished *adjective* ....
modern conveniences *noun* ....
reference *noun* ....
all inclusive *expression* ....
deposit *noun* ....
....
....
....

Reading B
tenancy *noun* ....
witness *noun* ....
tenant *noun* ....
landlord *noun* ....
property *noun* ....
term *noun* ....
rent *noun* ....
....
....
....

Unit**4**

Reading A
baggage *noun* ....
allowance *noun* ....
dimension *noun* ....
excess (baggage) *adjective* ....
overweight *adjective* ....
oversized *adjective* ....
....
....
....

Reading B
missing (items) *adjective* ....
trace *verb* ....
delayed (bags) *adjective* ....
destination *noun* ....
boarding card *noun* ....
baggage check label *noun* ....
....
....
....

Unit**5**

Reading A
mail *noun* ....
perishable *adjective* ....
postcode *noun* ....
packet *noun* ....
signature *noun* ....
evidence *noun* ....
on your behalf *expression* ....
proof *noun* ....
redeliver *verb* ....
....
....
....

Reading B
interrupt *verb* ....
guidance *noun* ....
restore *verb* ....
stop valve *noun* ....
....
....
....

Unit**6**

Reading A
bed and breakfast *noun* ....
spectacular *adjective* ....
en-suite *adjective* ....
excursion *noun* ....
sanctuary *noun* ....
proprietor *noun* ....
....
....
....

Reading B
tariff *noun* ....
settle *verb* ....
legally binding *expression* ....
liable *adjective* ....
insure *verb* ....
cancellation *noun* ....
ensure *verb* ....
....
....
....

Unit 7
Reading A
insider *noun* _____
congregate *verb* _____
dispersed *adjective* _____
impeccable *adjective* _____
top-notch *adjective* _____
perspective *noun* _____
dossier *noun* _____
tack on *verb* _____
adrenalin *noun* _____
_____
_____
_____

Reading B
charge *verb* _____
flimsy *adjective* _____
billow *verb* _____
twig *noun* _____
hurtle *verb* _____
wilderness *noun* _____
solitude *noun* _____
_____
_____
_____

Unit 8
Reading A
elusive *adjective* _____
standing *noun* _____
elude *verb* _____
offence *noun* _____
persistent *adjective* _____
endorse *verb* _____
obsessive *noun* _____
devote *verb* _____
portable *adjective* _____
reap rewards *collocation* _____
frame *noun* _____
manufacturing *noun* _____
_____
_____
_____

Reading B
overtake *verb* _____
psychologist *noun* _____
perception *noun* _____
predictable *adjective* _____
novice *noun* _____
offender *noun* _____
wig *noun* _____
caution *noun* _____
fatality *noun* _____
boom *noun* _____
hazard *noun* _____
collision *noun* _____
outweigh *verb* _____
_____
_____
_____

Unit 9
Reading A
prevent *verb* _____
threat *noun* _____
respect *verb* _____
lead *noun* _____
appliance *noun* _____
fire exit *noun* _____
fire door *noun* _____
fire drill *noun* _____
fire alarm *noun* _____
_____
_____
_____

Reading B
suspect *verb* _____
vicinity *noun* _____
intermittent *adjective* _____
continuous *adjective* _____
vacate *verb* _____
assembly point *noun* _____
_____
_____
_____

Unit 10
Reading A
marketing *noun* ....
folder *noun* ....
ship *verb* ....
cover *verb* ....
canteen *noun* ....
schedule *verb* ....
postpone *verb* ....
....
....
....
....

Reading B
emotion *noun* ....
resign *verb* ....
challenge *noun* ....
recruitment *noun* ....
promote *verb* ....
publicity *noun* ....
promotional item *noun* ....
invaluable *adjective* ....
supplier *noun* ....
maternity leave *noun* ....
....
....
....
....

Unit 11
Reading A
post *adjective* ....
vital *adjective* ....
satisfactory *adjective* ....
rate *verb* ....
picnic lunch *noun* ....
criticism *noun* ....
scale *noun* ....
scrutinize *verb* ....
hotelier *noun* ....
....
....
....

Reading B
feedback *noun* ....
booking *noun* ....
client *noun* ....
food poisoning *noun* ....
aspect *noun* ....
refurbish *verb* ....
remote *adjective* ....
....
....
....

Unit 12
Reading A
vacancy *noun* ....
handle *verb* ....
spreadsheet *noun* ....
database *noun* ....
enthusiasm *noun* ....
detail *noun* ....
accuracy *noun* ....
methodical *adjective* ....
initiative *noun* ....
deadline *noun* ....
....
....
....

Reading B
salary *noun* ....
probationary period *noun* ....
excess *noun* ....
annual leave *noun* ....
entitlement *noun* ....
remuneration *noun* ....
commencement *noun* ....
....
....
....

Unit 13
Reading A

GDP (gross domestic product) *noun* ....

bn (billion) *noun* ....

export *noun* ....

goods *noun* ....

financial services *noun* ....

construction *noun* ....

utilities *noun* ....

machinery *noun* ....

equipment *noun* ....

petroleum products *noun* ....

chemicals *noun* ....

manufactured goods *noun* ....

import *noun* ....

....

....

....

Reading B

etiquette *noun* ....

bear in mind *expression* ....

status *noun* ....

nickname *noun* ....

handshake *noun* ....

business card *noun* ....

protocol *noun* ....

counterpart *noun* ....

small talk *noun* ....

....

....

....

Unit 14
Reading A

thesaurus *noun* ....

encyclopaedia *noun* ....

alphabetical order *noun* ....

idiom *noun* ....

....

....

....

Reading B

simile *noun* ....

abbreviation *noun* ....

acronym *noun* ....

....

....

....

Unit 15
Reading A

catalogue *noun* ....

audio book *noun* ....

search *noun + verb* ....

mouse *noun* ....

return key *noun* ....

keyword *noun* ....

....

....

....

Reading B

cast *noun* ....

murder *noun* ....

suspect *noun* ....

corpse *noun* ....

strangle *verb* ....

....

....

Unit 16
Reading A

ability *noun* ....

technique *noun* ....

classify *verb* ....

recreational *adjective* ....

shift *verb* ....

provide *verb* ....

pay (close) attention to *expression* ....

flexibility *noun* ....

pattern *noun* ....

....

....

....

Reading B

process *noun* ....

memory *noun* ....

unfamiliar *adjective* ....

clue *noun* ....

prefix *noun* ....

suffix *noun* ....

....

....

....

Each unit of this book contains one *Learning tip*. However, this does not mean that this tip is useful in only that particular unit. Most *Learning tips* can be used in several different units. Here are all the *Learning tips* in the book. Each one is under its unit heading and you will also find a list of the types of text you read in that unit.

When you have completed a unit, decide which text you used the *Learning tip* with (this could be more than one text type). In addition, look at the other *Learning tips* and decide if you also used any of those tips in the unit you have just finished. Make a note of the unit name and number and the text type on the empty lines. In this way, you can keep a record of the reading strategies that you are developing.

Unit1 I'll cook something

Learning tip

We always read for a purpose. Sometimes this means that we do not need to read everything in front of us in order to find the information we are looking for. We can ignore some of the text.

A recipes ☐
B packaging ☐
   till receipt ☐

Which other units have you used this *Learning tip* in?

Unit2 We've hired a car

Learning tip

We sometimes search a text for a specific piece of information – this could be the answer to a question or simply a particular word or words. This type of reading is called scanning. When we scan, we do not read every word. We look quickly to find what we are looking for.
Scanning may be the first step in our reading of a text. Once we have found something we are looking for, we might go on to read the text around it.

A car rental voucher ☐
   webpage ☐
B rental instructions ☐

Which other units have you used this *Learning tip* in?

Unit3 Somewhere to live

Learning tip

The texts in this book are real texts written for ordinary people. These people read the texts with a purpose in mind – for example, people read accommodation advertisements like those in this unit because they want a place to live.
When you read a text, ask yourself: Who would read this text? Why would they read it? Understanding who would read something, and why, will help you to read the text as if you were reading it in the real world.

A advertisements ☐
B tenancy agreement ☐

Which other units have you used this *Learning tip* in?

Unit**4** I'll check it in

Learning tip

We usually look at a text quickly to find out what it is about. This type of reading is called skimming. When we skim, we get the main idea and don't pay attention to the small details. Skimming is very often the first step in reading a text.

A webpage ☐
    webpage ☐
B lost luggage form ☐

Which other units have you used this *Learning tip* in?

Unit**5** I'll be at home

Learning tip

We often skim a text the first time we read it – we read it quickly to get a general sense. Alternatively, we scan a text – we read it quickly to find a particular piece of information. After a quick read, we sometimes go back and read parts of the text more carefully to find out further, more detailed information. We can use any combination of these different reading skills to find the information we need.

A mail delivery card ☐
    webpage ☐
B leaflet ☐

Which other units have you used this *Learning tip* in?

Unit**6** A weekend in Wales

Learning tip

Think about what you already know about a topic before you read a text about it. This allows you to relate what you read to what you already know, and it makes the new text easier to understand.

A webpage ☐
B letter ☐

Which other units have you used this *Learning tip* in?

Unit**7** I saw an article about it

Learning tip

Journalists often begin factual magazine articles with dramatic true stories to catch the reader's attention. They give the factual information later. To tell these true stories, journalists might use direct speech, past tenses and personal pronouns (*I*, *he*, *we*, etc.). Look out for these things in an article and then you will be able to recognize which parts of it are the dramatic beginning and which parts give the factual information.

A magazine article ☐
B magazine article ☐

Which other units have you used this *Learning tip* in?

Unit **8** In the newspapers

Learning tip

Newspapers contain an enormous number and variety of reading texts, but most people do not read a newspaper from cover to cover. What we read depends on what we are interested in. We look at headlines, which summarize articles, and either read the article – part of it or all of it, again depending on our interest – or move on to another article. We read selectively.

A beginnings of newspaper articles ☐
B newspaper article ☐

Which other units have you used this _Learning tip_ in?

Unit **9** Let's go there

Learning tip

Dictionaries – both bilingual and monolingual – are very useful when you are learning a language. However, try not to use them too much. When you are reading, try to work out the meaning of an unknown word. Think about the other words around it, the word class it belongs to (e.g. noun, verb), similar words you know in English and similar words in your own language. Then use the dictionary to check that you have worked out the meaning of the word correctly.

A leaflet ☐
B notice ☐

Which other units have you used this _Learning tip_ in?

Unit **10** Lines of communication

Learning tip

When you read an email, find out who it is from and who it is for. Sometimes the message is just for you, sometimes it is for you as a member of a group, and sometimes you are copied in (cc = carbon copy, i.e. you are sent a copy of an email which has been sent primarily to someone else). If you know who the email has been sent to, you will know whether you have to reply, or take some kind of action.

A emails ☐
B emails ☐
  notices ☐

Which other units have you used this _Learning tip_ in?

Unit **11** Any comments?

Learning tip

Make sure you know the meaning of words and expressions used to link facts and ideas. This will help you to understand the meaning of the text and what the writer is saying. Here are some examples:

giving a reason	_because, since, as_
expressing a contrast	_whereas, otherwise, but, while, however, although_
expressing a result	_consequently, therefore, as a result_
rephrasing	_in other words, i.e._
giving an example	_for example, for instance, e.g._
adding something	_furthermore, in addition, also_

A questionnaire ☐
B report ☐

Which other units have you used this _Learning tip_ in?

Appendix 2 Learning tips

Unit 12 I'm going to apply

Learning tip

Most of our everyday correspondence, such as notes and emails, is in informal language. However, on some occasions we receive formal letters. The language used in these is serious and correct, and less like spoken language. One way of understanding the content of a formal letter is to put it into more neutral everyday language.

A job advertisement ☐
   part of a CV ☐
B letter of appointment ☐

Which other units have you used this *Learning tip* in?

Unit 13 I'm off on a trip

Learning tip

We don't only read texts. We also read visuals, such as tables, graphs and diagrams. Often these are a more direct way of presenting information than through text. Visuals sometimes have to be read with text, but at other times they stand alone. As with texts, we always read them with a purpose and that is to extract meaning.

A webpages ☐
B webpage ☐

Which other units have you used this *Learning tip* in?

Unit 14 Look it up!

Learning tip

We use reference books for finding specific pieces of information. Each double page of an alphabetically ordered reference book has two words in bold at the top of the pages. These show the first and last entries on those two pages. Our knowledge of the alphabet helps us to scan the reference book to find the words we are looking for.

A reference book entries ☐
B introduction to a book of facts ☐
   headings in a book of facts ☐
   entries from a book of facts ☐

Which other units have you used this *Learning tip* in?

Unit 15 It's on the shelf

Learning tip

Reading whole articles, stories and books is a good way to improve your extensive reading skills so that reading for study becomes easier.
When you go to a bookshop or library, choose books that you are interested in. Skim two or three pages and make sure there are not too many new words (a maximum of ten per page). If there are more, you won't be able to work out their meaning from the other words in the text. Direct speech breaks up the text and is generally easier than narrative or descriptive writing.
When you start reading, don't stop in the middle of a sentence or paragraph and go back – continue until the end of a page or chapter.

A webpages ☐
B novel extract ☐

Which other units have you used this *Learning tip* in?

Unit 16 Read about reading

> ### Learning tip
>
> When we read a long text for the first time, we usually skim it in order to find out the general meaning and to identify the parts which we want to read in detail. The most important parts of the text are the first paragraph, which introduces the overall topic, and the first sentence of each of the other paragraphs. This sentence usually introduces the topic of the paragraph.

A encyclopaedia extract ☐
B encyclopaedia extract ☐

Which other units have you used this _Learning tip_ in?

Appendix3
Using a dictionary

What kind of dictionary should I use?

If possible, you should use two dictionaries: a good bilingual dictionary (in both your own language and with English translations) and a good monolingual dictionary (English words with English definitions). A monolingual dictionary may give you more information about a word or phrase; in addition, it is a good idea for you to work in English as much as possible. The examples on these pages are from the *Cambridge Learner's Dictionary*.

What information can I find in a dictionary?

The most common reason for looking a word up in a dictionary is to find out its meaning. However, a dictionary can also give you a lot of other information about a word. The *Cambridge Learner's Dictionary*, for example, can give up to six types of information before the meaning of the word and two further types of information after it. The words in the following examples are all from Unit 1.

1 the base form of the word

Each entry begins with the base form of the word.

> **yolk** /jəʊk/ *noun* [C] the round, yellow part in the middle of an egg

2 the pronunciation of the word

These symbols show you how to say the word.

> **sieve** /sɪv/ *noun* [C] a piece of kitchen equipment with a wire or plastic net which separates large pieces of food from liquids or powders *Pass the sauce through a sieve to remove any lumps.* ➲See colour picture **The Kitchen** on page Centre 2. • **sieve** *verb* [T]

3 its part of speech

This tells you what part of speech – noun, verb, adjective, etc. – a word is.

> **partially** /ˈpɑːʃ°li/ *adverb* not completely *partially cooked*

4 any special grammatical features of the word

[**often passive**] shows that the passive form (modified) of this verb is often used

> **modify** /'mɒdɪfaɪ/ *verb* [T] **1** to change something in order to improve it [**often passive**] *The plans will have to be modified to reduce costs.* ○ *genetically modified food*

5 irregular past tense forms, plural nouns and comparatives/superlatives

Plurals which are not regular are shown.

> ○━**leaf**¹ /liːf/ *noun* [C] *plural* **leaves** /liːvz/ **1** a flat, green part of a **plant that grows from a stem or branch** *an oak leaf*

6 whether the word is only used in British English (UK) or American English (US)

UK means that a word is only used in British English; *US* means that a word is used only in American English.

> **aubergine** /'əʊbəʒiːn/ *UK* (*US* **eggplant**) *noun* [C, U] an oval, purple vegetable that is white inside

7 the meaning of the word

> **packaging** /'pækɪdʒɪŋ/ *noun* [U] the paper, box, etc that something is inside so that it can be sold or sent somewhere

The definition tells you what the word means.

8 example phrases or sentences

> **roam** /rəʊm/ *verb* [I, T] to move around a place without any purpose *gangs of youths* **roaming the street** *at night*

Examples (in *italics*) can show you how a word is used in a phrase/sentence.

9 other words this word goes with (collocations)

> ○━**mix**¹ /mɪks/ *verb* **1** COMBINE SUBSTANCES [I, T] If two or more substances mix, they combine to more substances, you combine them to make one substance. ***Mix** the powder **with** water to form a paste.* ○ *Put the chocolate, butter, and egg in a bowl and* ***mix** them all **together**.*

Words in **bold** in an example show you which words are often used together.

How should I use my dictionary?

1   At the top of each page in the *Cambridge Learner's Dictionary*, there is a word in **bold** black type. The word in the top left corner of the left page is the first word on this page; the word in the top right corner of the right page is the last word on this page. If you are looking for the word **sponge**, it will be between the two words **split** (top left corner of the left page) and **spread** (top right corner of the right page).

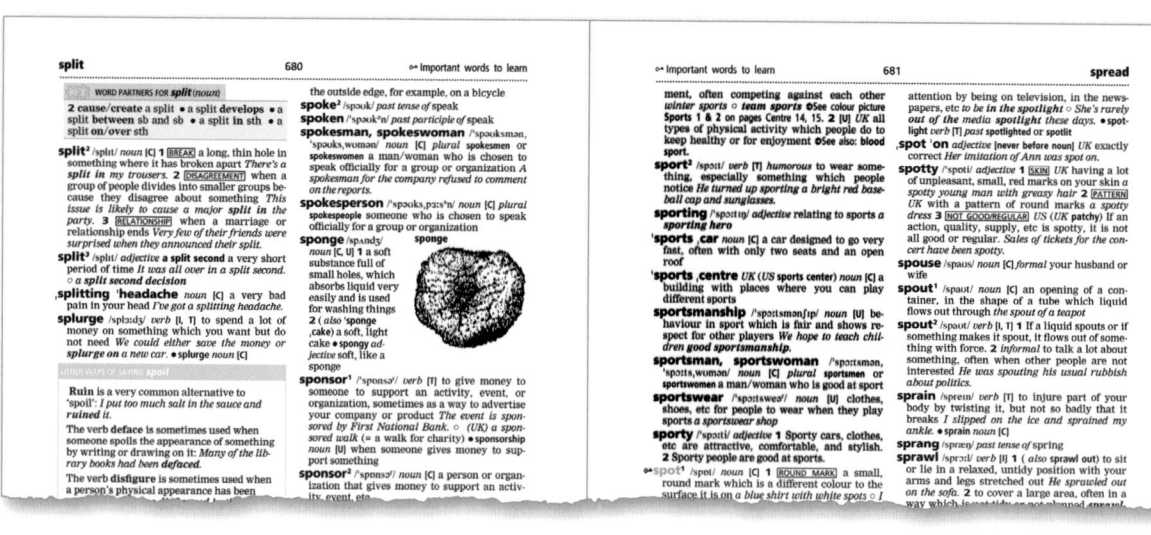

2   Each time you look up a word, you could use a highlighter pen to mark the word in your dictionary. When you return to a page with a highlighter mark, look at the word quickly and check that you remember its meaning.

savour *UK* (*US* **savor**) /'seɪvəʳ/ *verb* [T] to enjoy food or a pleasant experience as much and as slowly as possible *to savour a meal* ○ *I ate slowly, savouring every mouthful.* ○ *We savoured our moment of victory.*

savoury *UK* (*US* **savory**) /'seɪvºri/ *adjective* Savoury food is not sweet. *savoury biscuits* ○ *Generally, I prefer savoury to sweet food.*

savvy /'sævi/ *noun* [U] *informal* practical knowledge and ability *business/political savvy* ● **savvy** *adjective informal* having knowledge and ability *a savvy consumer*

3   A word in your dictionary may not be exactly the same as its form in the text you are reading. This is because the word in the text may be: a plural form of a noun; a comparative or superlative form of an adjective; a verb ending in *-s*, *-ed*, *-ing*; or an irregular form of a verb, e.g. *minced.*

mince¹ /mɪns/ *UK* (*US* **ground beef**) *noun* [U] meat, usually from a cow, which has been cut into very small pieces by a machine

mince² /mɪns/ *verb* [T] to cut food into small pieces in a machine *minced beef/onions*

mincemeat /'mɪnsmiːt/ *noun* [U] **1** a spicy, sweet mixture of apples, dried fruit, and nuts, which have been cut into small pieces **2 make mincemeat of sb** *informal* to defeat someone very easily

mince 'pie *noun* [C] *UK* a small pastry filled with mincemeat that is eaten mainly at Christmas

A headword is the word whose meaning is explained.

4 The words that are defined in the dictionary are called headwords. Sometimes a headword can have more than one meaning. The first meaning in the dictionary is not always the one you want. Read through the different meanings and decide which one is correct in this context.

clove /kləʊv/ *noun* [C] **1** a small, dark-brown, dried flower that is used as a spice **2** one separate part in a root of garlic (= plant with a strong taste used in cooking)

A guideword helps you find the meaning you want.

5 Words which have several meanings sometimes have guidewords to help you find the meaning you are looking for. Usually the most common meaning appears first. The first meaning in the dictionary is not always the one you want. Read through the different meanings and decide which one is correct in this context.

grain /greɪn/ *noun* **1** SEED [C, U] a seed or seeds from types of grass which are eaten as food *grains of wheat/rice* **2** PIECE [C] a very small piece of something *a grain of sand/sugar* **3** QUALITY [no plural] a very small amount of a quality *There isn't **a grain of truth** in her story.* **4 the grain** the natural direction and pattern of lines which you can see in wood or material *to cut something along/against the grain* **5 go against the grain** If something goes against the grain, you would not normally do it because it would be unusual or morally wrong. ⟳See also: take sth with a pinch of **salt**[1].

6 Some words in your dictionary may have more than one headword. (Small numbers after the headword will indicate this.) This is because the word can be used as different parts of speech – for example, an adjective and a noun. The part of speech of the unknown word should be clear from the context (the words around it).

○━**medium**[1] /ˈmiːdiəm/ *adjective* in the middle of a group of different amounts or sizes *people of medium weight* ○ *She bought a **medium-sized** car.* ○ *The shirt comes in small, medium, and large.*
medium[2] /ˈmiːdiəm/ *noun* [C] *plural* **media** or **mediums** a way of communicating or expressing something *the medium of television/radio* ○ *The Internet has become yet another **medium** for marketing.*

7 Dictionaries are particularly helpful with the meaning of phrasal verbs and idioms since their meaning is different from the meaning of the separate parts. You will find phrasal verbs, idioms and other expressions after all the other definitions of the word.

When should I use my dictionary?

A dictionary is very useful when you are learning a foreign language. However, when you are reading, do not use your dictionary too much. Using your dictionary will interrupt your reading and slow you down. In your own language, you don't always understand the meaning of every word; it is not necessary to understand everything in English either.

1 When you see an English word that you don't know, first try to guess the meaning of the word from its context (the words around it). You may find another word with a similar meaning, a word which means the opposite, or some words which actually explain the unknown word. Only use your dictionary to check your guess.

2 The only other time you should look a word up in your dictionary is if there are no clues in the text and you are sure the unknown word is important.

Answer**key**

Unit 1

A

1 The third recipe (pasta with aubergine and mozzarella sauce) uses tinned (canned) tomatoes, garlic and Parmesan cheese.

Focus on verbs

b shred   c de-seed   d dice   e crush   f grate
g peel   h stone

2 To make pasta with aubergine and mozzarella sauce you also need:
an onion, an aubergine, a 400g can of chopped tomatoes, salt and black pepper, fresh basil, 150g mozzarella cheese, Parmesan cheese and 400g pasta.
3 b T   c F   d F   e F
4 You also need: coffee, 3 eggs, 250g mascarpone, sugar, cocoa powder.

B

2 Pasta with aubergine and mozzarella sauce: 3a and 3b, 4a and 4b, 6a and 6b
Tiramisù: 2a and 2b, 5a and 5b

3

	Ingredient	Advantages	Disadvantages
2a	large eggs	large, can keep until 30 June	hens live indoors
2b	medium eggs	hens free outside, hens fed on GM-free food	slightly more expensive, can only keep until 27 June
3a	black peppercorns	gives fresh black pepper	you need a pepper mill
3b	ground black pepper	you don't need a pepper mill	not fresh, more expensive
4a	fresh grated Parmigiano Reggiano	fresh and grated, from Italy, extra mature (i.e. strong)	expensive
4b	grated Italian hard cheese	much cheaper	partially dried (i.e. not fresh), not Parmesan cheese
5a	coffee beans	gives fresh coffee	you need a coffee grinder
5b	coffee filters	you don't need a coffee grinder	expensive for 10 cups of coffee
6a	Italian plum tomatoes	exact weight needed, Italian tomatoes	need chopping
6b	Quality chopped tomatoes	already chopped, packaging has advantages over a can	slightly under weight needed

4 There are no right and wrong answers. It depends on what your priorities are, for example: cost, quality, preparation time or equipment needed.
5 The shopper chose: quality chopped tomatoes, wholewheat penne, medium eggs, ground black pepper, grated Parmesan and the coffee filters. Again, there are no right and wrong answers – you are just reading in order to compare with your product choices.
6 The shopper also bought the following ingredients for the two dishes: sugar, sponge fingers, cocoa powder, mozzarella, aubergine, basil, onions and salt.

Unit2

Get ready to read

- *Your own answers.*
- *Your own answers.*
- Cape Town, Durban and Johannesburg are in South Africa. (Abuja is in Nigeria and Nairobi is in Kenya.)

A

1 They are collecting the car from Cape Town and they are returning it to Johannesburg.

2 c

3 They have paid for six extras: 1 CDW, 2 PAI, 3 TLW, 4 UM, 5 Tax, 6 Surcharge.

4 a CDW, PAI, TLW and Surcharge are explained in detail. Tax is mentioned but not explained in detail. UM is not explained.
  b CDW stands for Collision Damage Waiver.
    PAI stands for Personal Accident Insurance.
    TLW stands for Theft Loss Waiver.
  c UM stands for Unlimited Mileage. This means that the rental fee doesn't depend on how far you drive.

5 They have to pay a 1% tourism levy, a rental contract fee of ZAR 30.78 and 14% VAT (Value Added Tax). They do not have to pay the 9% airport surcharge because they are not collecting their car at an airport.

6 They will pay more as SCDW means that the renter pays a 'reduced excess', i.e. pays a lower sum of money towards the cost of the claim.

7 *Your own answers. Possible answer*:
  I would probably buy Limited Cover accident insurance because I'm quite an experienced driver and I've never had an accident before. I might buy Super Cover theft insurance as I usually travel with lots of luggage. I suppose it also depends which country I'm going to drive in.

B

1 Yes, they should keep the envelope because they need to add some information to it and return it to Avis at the end of their trip.

2 You'll need to carry cash because in South Africa you can't use credit cards to pay for petrol.

3 b We have to wear our seat belts all the time.
  c We have to drive on the left-hand side of the road.
  d We have to obey speed limits.

4 b We should shut windows and lock all doors and the boot when we're not in the car.
  c We shouldn't leave personal belongings in the car.
  d We should use the immobiliser when we're not in the car.

5 They should check the tyres regularly.

6 The most useful number is +27 (0)800 001 669. This is the number they should call if their car breaks down or if they have a medical emergency.

Focus on vocabulary

b vehicle c tyre d immobiliser e fuel gauge
f driver's licence g seat belt h speed limit
i unleaded petrol

Unit3

Get ready to read

- *Your own answers.*
- *Your own answers.*

A

1 *Your own answers. Possible answers*:
  How much does it cost per week/month?
  Is it non-smoking?
  Is it in a house with other people who are renting, or is it in a family home?
  Is there somewhere for my car/bike?
  Is it near public transport?
  How long is it available for?

2 *Your own answers. Possible answers for the above questions are*:
  1 The price is in all four advertisements.
  2 The room in advertisement a is non-smoking.
  3 The room in advertisement a is in a house with other people who are renting. The room in advertisement d is in a family home. Advertisements b and c do not say if the rooms are in a house where other people rent or if they are in a family home.
  4 Advertisement c mentions 'off-road parking', i.e. a place, such as a drive in front of the house or a parking space, where you can park your car off the road. None of the advertisements mentions bikes.
  5 None of the advertisements mentions public transport.
  6 Advertisement c says that the rooms are available for eight months. Advertisement d says the room can be rented long or short term. The other advertisements don't mention how long the rooms are available. They are probably available for as long as you want them.

3 The advertisements are more difficult to understand because they contain a lot of abbreviations (short forms), e.g. 'sgl rm' is an abbreviation for 'single room'.

4 e sgl rm: single room
    nr: near
    f n/s: female non-smoker
    pcm all incl: per calendar month all inclusive (i.e. you do not pay extra for bills, such as electricity, gas)
    avail beg Jan: available beginning (of) January
  f mins: minutes
    d/g + gas c/h: double glazing and gas central heating
    ASAP: as soon as possible
    mths: months

Refs req.: references required (i.e. you need a letter from an employer or a teacher which says that you are an honest and reliable person)

g 1 bed: one-bedroom

furn: furnished

prof couple: professional couple (i.e. married couple or couple living together who work rather than are students)

mod cons: modern conveniences (i.e. modern equipment, such as central heating, a dishwasher, washing machine and dryer)

pcm excl bills: per calendar month excluding bills (i.e. you have to pay extra for bills, such as electricity, gas)

eves: evenings

h dbl rm: double room

m owner: male owner

pw incl bills: per week including bills (i.e. you do not pay extra for bills, such as electricity, gas) (Note that £70 per week is more expensive than £280 per month, since most months contain 30 or 31 days.)

5 *Your own answers. Possible answers*:

Julia: the most suitable room is the room in advertisement d. Julia wants to live with a British family. She is only going to be in Cambridge for two months and the room is available long or short term.

Marina and **Stefan**: the most suitable accommodation is the flat in advertisement g. Marina is a professional (she works as a teacher), and they don't particularly want to share accommodation with other people.

Pei Lan: the most suitable room is the room in advertisement f. Pei Lan visits her friends in London, so living near the railway station will be convenient. Also, we can assume that the advertisements appeared on the Internet or in the newspaper in December or January since advertisement c and advertisement e say that rooms are available in January. This means that Pei Lan needs a room for six months – and the room in advertisement f is available for six months.

Ibrahim: the most suitable room is one of the rooms in advertisement c. Ibrahim has a car. In addition, his cousin, who is arriving soon, could rent the other room.

Mirella: the most suitable room is the room in advertisement e. Mirella is a female non-smoker. A room near the city centre would be useful for her, since she can't drive. This is a single room and Mirella is happy to rent a small room. The advertisement doesn't say that all the other people are women, but we know that one of them is. This is Jane, the person who you should contact if you're interested in the room.

Tolga: the most suitable room is the room in advertisement h. Tolga has a car. He would like a larger room than the one he currently has, so a double room should suit him.

Aleksy: the most suitable room is the room in advertisement a. Aleksy doesn't want to pay more than £60 a week, and this room is £225 per calendar month. In addition, he doesn't want to live on his own or with a family – and this room is in a mixed shared house.

6 *Your own answer. Possible answer*:

I would be most interested in the room in Chesterton because it is large and in a shared house. I would like to live with other people and improve my English in this way.

B

1 a Marina (Kahn) signed the agreement.

b The agreement is for the property in Advertisement g.

c Alice Race witnessed Marina's signature.

d Alice is a secondary school teacher, perhaps in the school where Marina teaches German. Alice lives in Cambridge.

2 b 15 March c two d won't e must

3 b 8 c 1 d 4 e 10 f 2 g 5 h 6 i 9 j 3

4 a yes (point 2) b yes (point 1) c no (point 7)
d yes (point 2) e yes (point 4) f no (point 8)

Focus on formal language

b beginning c warning d tell e used
f agreement g outside

Unit4

Get ready to read

○ b suitcase c holdall d vanity case
e garment bag f briefcase

○ *Your own answer.*

A

1 Yes, this is the webpage he needs.

2 The webpage gives information about a, b and c.

3 a maximum linear dimensions 158 cm, e.g. 80 cm long, 48 cm high, 30 cm wide

b 46 kg

4 You have to pay an excess baggage fee when you have too many bags, or when your bags are too big or too heavy.

5 $70 CAD

6 b Y c N d N

7 *Your own answers. Possible answer*:

No, I've never paid an excess baggage fee.

Focus on the prefix *over*

b overgrown c overdue d overcrowded
e overrated f overpriced

B

1 *Your own answer. Possible answer*:
I think he should tell someone from the airline that his luggage hasn't arrived.

2 b 5 c 2 d 3 e 7 f 1 g 9 h 6 i 4

3 Yes, he should be optimistic. The introduction says that most delayed bags are found and returned to their owner within 48 hours.

4

Missing items

Dear Customer

We are sorry that your baggage was mishandled during your recent flight and would be grateful if you could complete the form below to assist us in tracing it.

We would like to assure you that every effort will be made to locate your baggage and return it to you as soon as possible. We are pleased to report that the vast majority of delayed bags are found and returned to their owners within 48 hours.

If your baggage has not been located within 48 hours, we will continue to trace it for a maximum of three months.

PLEASE WRITE CLEARLY USING BLOCK CAPITALS

NAME: Miklós Pilzinsky

ADDRESS AT DESTINATION: 12–111 CARLTON TOWER ROAD, TORONTO, ONTARIO M4C 5L6

TELEPHONE/MOBILE NUMBER: (001) 416 333 4276

DATE OF TRAVEL: 26 NOV

FROM: PARIS, CHARLES DE GAULLE TO: TORONTO, LESTER B PEARSON INTERNATIONAL

FLIGHT NUMBER: AIR CANADA 854   BAGGAGE CHECK NUMBER: 0014 AC790278

TYPE OF ITEM	SIZE	COLOUR
HOLDALL	LARGE	BLUE
HARDSHELL SUITCASE	MEDIUM	RED

Signature Miklós Pilzinsky   Date 26th Nov

Unit5

Get ready to read

○ *Your own answers.*
○ *Your own answers.*

A

1 a The card is from Royal Mail, i.e. the postman.
 b The card is for Raquel Ramos García.
 c The card has been put through Raquel's door because she was out when the postman called.

2 b How to get your item

3 a going back to the Delivery Office   b 2.32 pm

4 b F ('If someone's collecting on your behalf, they'll need to provide proof of your identity.')
 c F (You have to phone – or go online – if you want Redelivery or 'Local Collect' services.)
 d F ('We can Redeliver to your address or to an alternative local address.' No fee is mentioned.)
 e T ('Or for 50p you can have your item taken to a local Post Office® Branch for you to pick up using our "Local Collect" service.')
 f F ('Please note we'll keep a Recorded item for 1 week, and all other items for 3 weeks before returning them to the sender.')

5 b (Sam Williams lives in the same postcode area as Raquel: RG24.)

Class bonus

Your own answers. Possible answers:
Maybe Raquel is out at work/college every day of the week, or she doesn't know when she'll be at home.
Perhaps she doesn't live near a post office (so she doesn't want to use the 'Local Collect' service) or near the Royal Mail Delivery Office (to collect the item).
She probably decides to have it redelivered to her friend's house because he told her that he would be at home on Wednesday.

B

1 a The leaflet is from Thames Water.
 b It is for everyone who uses water – in this case, Raquel and anyone else who lives in her house.
 c It has been put through the door to inform residents that their water supply will be interrupted for two hours on Saturday morning.

2 a, c and d

3 b can't c can't d can't e can

4 a 7 b 2 c 4 d 1 e 9 f 3 g 6 h 8
 i 5 j 10

Focus on phrasal verbs

b Switch c turning
Switch off and *turn off* have the same meaning. *Cut off*, in this context, means 'to stop providing water'. Only Thames Water can cut off the water.
The following sentences are also correct: d, e, g, i, j, k.

Unit6

Get ready to read

○ a Scotland b England c Wales
 d Northern Ireland
○ The sentences are all true apart from a. The national sport of Wales is rugby.

A

1 Geraint is recommending St David's. (Note that Geraint is a Welsh name, so he is probably from Wales or his family is originally Welsh.)

2 b On the Coast Path you can see lots of birds and flowers.
 c The beaches are some of the safest and cleanest in Europe.
 d There are birds on three sanctuary islands: Ramsey, Skomer and Skokholm.

3 b Ramsey House c St David's d picnic lunches
 e drying room f en-suite g every room
 h secure bicycle storage

4 b N ('Situated within walking distance of St David's')
 c Y ('private off-road parking')
 d N ('exclusively for adults')

5 *Your own answer. Possible answer*:
I'd like to stay there because the bedrooms and garden sound nice. Also, I'd like the homemade bread for breakfast.

B

1 *Your own answers. Possible answers*:
b Have you got two twin rooms?
c How much are they?
d What time are the rooms available from?
e Can we pay by credit card?
f What time do we have to leave on our last day?

2 The letter is from Ceri Morgan, one of the proprietors of Ramsey House.

3 *Your own answers. Possible answers*:
b Yes, two twin rooms are available.
c The rooms are £35 per person per night.
d The rooms are available from 2.00 pm on the day of arrival.
e No, bills can only be paid by cheque or in cash.
f Guests have to leave after breakfast on the day of departure.

4 b He paid by cheque.
c They will have to pay £280 more.
d They can either pay by cheque or in cash.

5 c ('We have pleasure in reserving etc.')
d ('Should you cancel … cost of your holiday.')
e ('You may … insurance.')

6 a The proprietors might keep the money.
b Yes, they might have to pay the rest, i.e. £280 more, because they are 'liable for a cancellation charge up to the total cost of your holiday'.
c They would get their money back if the proprietors re-let the accommodation, i.e. if some other guests used their rooms.
d Yes, if he had holiday insurance, this would (probably) pay any cancellation charges he had.

7 *Your own answers. Possible answer*:
They will probably re-let the rooms because the bed and breakfast and the area sound very nice. The end of May is almost summer and it is a popular time for trips. Some people might just ring the doorbell rather than phone in advance. However, Sebastian has cancelled very late, so there isn't much time for them to re-let. Also, they might not re-let if the weather isn't very nice.

Focus on *should*

b Should you see anyone in danger
c Should we be out
d Should you leave anything behind
e Should you change your mind
f Should the telephone ring
g Should you require refreshments
h Should the weather worsen

Unit7

Get ready to read

○ *Your own answers.*
◐ *Your own answers.*

A

1 The article is from a travel magazine.
2 You can see some tourists on safari. They are in a 4WD (four-wheel drive) vehicle. The animal is a cheetah.
3 a 2 b 4 c 3 d 5 e 1
4 b W c W d W e D f W
5 *Your own answers. Possible answers*:
b If you stay in a lodge, you will have luxury accommodation and you will be very comfortable.
c If you go on a game drive, you can travel to different places and see different animals.
d If you go on a walking safari, you can go to places that most people don't go to, you can see smaller animals and you can listen to the quieter sounds.
e If you go on a boat, you can see animals at waterholes and in rivers.
6 b South Africa c Zambia d Kenya e Tanzania
7 *Your own answers. Possible answers*:
a I'd prefer to camp.
b I'd like to go to East Africa to see the Great Migration.
c I'd like to go on a walking safari for some of the time.
d I'd like to climb Kilimanjaro, so I'd go to Tanzania.
e I'd have to go in July, August or September if I wanted to see the Great Migration.

Focus on vocabulary

b lodge c trail d the bush e species f ape

B

1 'A walk in the park' is something that is easy to do.
2 The walk is in Kruger National Park. (This is in South Africa.)
3 c
4 She ends the dramatic beginning in paragraph 5. 'It's the kind of encounter people dream of – and dread – when they do a wilderness trail.'
5 Paragraph 6 is about wilderness trails and areas in Kruger National Park in general.
Paragraph 7 is about the Olifants Trail Camp.
6 She saw the rhino on the second morning. (On the map, the small drawing of the rhino is near the dashed lines which indicate the second morning walk.)
7 a 3 b 1 c 6 d 2 e 5 f 4

8 *Your own answers. Possible answers*:
People want to see animals in the wild – but they don't want the animals to attack them. I would have been frightened when the rhino charged.

9 They would have used their guns. Nicol says he has done this twice – against elephants. He did this because he was responsible for a group of walkers. He wouldn't have done it if he'd been on his own.

10 *Your own answer. Possible answer*:
I'd like to go on a walk in the bush, but I'm not very keen on camping. A friend told me that there are about five main rest camps in Kruger National Park, where you can rent a bungalow. From these rest camps, you can go on a short walk in the bush early in the morning. You can also go on a bike ride!

Unit8

Get ready to read

○ *Your own answer.*
○ *Your own answers.*
○ *Your own answers.*

A

1 *Your own answers. Possible answers*:
Culture and Review: An article in this section could be about a new book or film about a famous cyclist.
Sport: An article in this section could be about a race, for example the Tour de France.
News: An article in this section could be about an increase in the number of bikes that are stolen or about an increase in the number of cycle paths.
Financial and Business: An article in this section could be about a company that makes bikes or about postmen who use bicycles.
Health and Medical: An article in this section could be about the benefits of cycling regularly or about the pollution risks of cycling in cities.
Travel: An article in this section could be about cycling holidays or about touring bikes.

2 Extract 1 – Sport
Extract 2 – News
Extract 3 – Financial and Business

3 a she has had a very successful season
b people who frequently cycle
c a long time

4 *Your own answer. Possible answer*:
I think 'Cooke shows ingredients for big prize' is the most difficult article to read. There are some words I don't know (*elusive*, *phenomenal*) and some other words are confusing. Some of the sentences are very long. My biggest problem is that I don't know any background information because I don't know anything about this person or the sport of cycling.

5 *Your own answers. Possible answers*:
1 Cooke is number 1 in women's cycling. She could win the World Championship this week. She has never won it.
2 A law might be introduced in the UK which would mean that you have to have a bell on your bike when you cycle. Cycling without one would be a criminal offence.
3 Andrew Ritchie has spent 30 years building a portable bike. He has sold nearly 100,000 bikes and his company is a manufacturing success.

6 *Your own answer. Possible answer*:
I'd rather choose an article of my own. I like sport, but I'd rather read about football.

B

1 b cycle path c lights d cycle panniers
e fluorescent jacket

2 Cyclists should do everything except b and e.

3 *Your own answer. Possible answer*:
Yes, the headline surprises me – I expected the second half of the headline to say 'more likely to be safe' or 'more likely to survive accidents'.

4 Sentence 2 gives more details about the main topic and gives a reason for the behaviour described in the main topic.
Sentence 3 gives contrasting information.

5

Where?	Salisbury and Bristol
How?	a bicycle fitted with an ultrasonic distance sensor which recorded data from more than 2,500 overtaking motorists
Why?	to find out how close overtaking vehicles got to cyclists – with and without helmets – and to raise awareness of the dangers facing cyclists on busy roads

6 b more experienced.
c female cyclists.
d Buses and trucks.
e increased to 148.
f beat congestion, reduce pollution and get fit.
g surviving if they are hit by a car.

7 *Your own answer. Possible answer*:
I'm very surprised to learn that vehicles drive much closer to cyclists who wear helmets and closer to men rather than to women. I'd never thought about these things before. I'm also shocked at the number of cyclists who died in accidents. This seems a very high number.

8 *Your own answer. Possible answer*:
No, cyclists shouldn't stop wearing helmets. Cyclists who wear helmets are more likely to survive a collision with a car than those who don't.

Focus on synonyms

fatalities, deaths

b hit – struck	injured – hurt
c overtaking – passing	carrying out – doing
d room – space	boom – increase
e perception – thought	data – figures (in article)
f rose – increased	suspected – believed
g test – experiment	risk – danger (in article)
h collision – accident	caution – care

Review1

A 1 F **2** T **3** T **4** F **5** T **6** F **7** F **8** T
C 9 D **10** B **11** A1 and A2 **12** C
D

		Cocoa powder	Drinking chocolate
13	This product already contains sugar.		✓
14	This product weighs less than the other.	✓	
15	You need more of this product to make a drink.		✓
16	You need to use some cold milk to make this drink.	✓	
17	This product costs less.		✓

E 18 More **19** can't **20** more **21** have to / must
22 half
F 23 F **24** T **25** T **26** F **27** T
G 28 e **29** b **30** a **31** d **32** c
H 33 b
I 34 a **35** b **36** f **37** h
J 38 lots of people were looking for accommodation
39 you don't want to have to buy furniture
40 you're working
41 weren't
42 their price
43 were able to
K 44 c
45 a
L 46 A
47–49
– because it is only a short walk from the beach and in the text Amanda says that they have a sea view (if on tiptoes).
– because it is much cheaper than the other one and in the text Amanda mentions that good value rental properties (for a two-bedroom flat) start at $360 (just above this price).

– because flat B says only people with permanent positions need apply and in the text it says that Amanda and Mark had no work lined up.
M 50 A and B
51 A
52 A
53 A and B
54 B
55 A

Unit9

Get ready to read

○ *Your own answers.*
○ a alarm b brigade c drill d exit
○ b 1 c 5 d 3 e 6 f 4

A

1 *Your own answers. Possible answers*:
Switch off computers when you are not using them.
Don't use portable heaters.
Store dangerous materials safely.
2 *Your own answers.* (The leaflet mentions the first and third points above.)
3 b 4 c 3 d 5 e 1
4 b 1 c 4 d 5 e 2
5 2 A fire door is a heavy door inside a building which prevents fire from spreading to other areas of the building.
3 A fire drill is the set of actions that people do to leave a building that is on fire.
4 A fire alarm is the bell or other signal that warns people there is a fire.

B

1 drill
2 suspect = think
intermittent = stopping for a short time and then starting again
(It is the opposite of *continuous* in the third heading.)
3 An alarm call point is a bell on the wall that sounds the fire alarm and also calls the fire brigade. An assembly point is a place where people meet.
Point here means 'a particular place'.
4 *Your own answers.*
5 a 1 b 2 c 1 d 3

Focus on compound nouns

b firefighter c firearm d firewood e fireplace
f firewall

6 b You should use the stairs to get to the ground floor and then go to assembly point 1.
   c You should take your mobile phone with you.
   d You should leave your sports bag under your desk.
   e You should check that no one is still in the area, for example, in the toilets.
   f You should check that everyone from your department is there.
   g You should report this to the Person in Control.

Unit 10

Get ready to read

○ *Your own answers.*
○ *Your own answers.*

A

1 a This is from Emma Wright – and it is to Isabel and Dan Vettori.
   b This is from Rotha Lim – and it is to Emma and Isabel. (Ben Parker is also copied in.)
   c This is from Dan Vettori – and it is to Isabel.
2 Email a gives some information.
   Email b requests something.
   Email c makes a suggestion.
3 Email a gives information about a cancelled meeting.
   Email b requests help with making conference folders the following week.
   Email c suggests an alternative date for a cancelled meeting.
4 d This is from Emma Wright – and it is to Paul Collingwood, Rotha Lim, Greg Kawana, Jane Reed and Dan Vettori.
   e This is from Emma – and it is to Paul.
   f This is from Emma – and it is to Jane, Rotha and Greg.
5 e She has been copied in so that she knows Paul is aware that she will collect the food and take it to the meeting.
   f She has been copied in so that she knows Jane, Rotha and Greg are aware she will attend the team meeting.

Focus on collocations

a cancel b schedule c postpone d meeting room
e team meeting

6 Email e suggests a possible reason – Paul is involved in a working lunch with five other people (perhaps visitors) on the following Monday. His meeting may start in the morning, which means that he is unable to attend the team meeting. In addition, Isabel needs to provide the food for the working lunch, so she wouldn't be able to go to the team meeting either.

7 Paul: working lunch – Monday; team meeting – Tuesday morning
   Rotha: team meeting – Tuesday morning; conference folders – one afternoon
   Greg: team meeting – Tuesday morning; trip to Auckland – Wednesday to Friday with Dan
   Jane: back to work; team meeting – Tuesday morning; meeting with Isabel and Dan – Tuesday afternoon perhaps
   Dan: team meeting – Tuesday morning; meeting with Jane and Isabel – Tuesday afternoon perhaps; trip to Auckland – Wednesday to Friday with Greg

B

1 a It's from Paul.
   b It's to Jane, Rotha, Greg, Dan and Isabel.
   c It's about Emma.
2 c
3 a company
   b at the end of the next week
   c for three years
4 a 4 b 2 c 1 d 5 e 3
5 a Office Administrator.
   b She deals with the website, the database, publicity and promotional items.
   c Temporary keyboard operator and administration assistant.
   d Recruitment Administrator at Lynams in Napier.
6 *Your own answers.*
7 Events a and f are true for Emma. There will be coffee and cakes at 4.30 pm next Friday (the day she's leaving) and then a meal at a Chinese restaurant for those who are able to and want to go.
8 No, this is not a leaving notice. Vincent Ingram is the new Office Administrator. He has been given Emma's old job.
9 b paragraph 4
   c paragraph 1
   d paragraph 3
10 *Your own answer. Possible answer:*
   I don't know whether he will enjoy working at Bishops. However, he has worked there before and chosen to go back, so he must have liked it before.

Unit 11

A

1 b Kranjska Gora, Lake Bohinj and Lake Bled.
   c The Vila Orel, the Turist Hotel and the Hotel Bella Vista.
   d Yes.

2 a, b

3 a negative   b positive

4 1 everyday we got the same boring cheese roll
   2 there is no lift

5 a (They only pass on comments where appropriate. They only let the client know what they have done in response to the comment if the client ticks a box.)

6 *Your own answer. Possible answer:*
They might discuss the issue of the picnics with the managers of the Vila Orel and the Turist Hotel.

7 b Positive
   c Positive
   d Negative – they could investigate the possibility of using the Hotel Julija in the village of Bohinj.
   e Mainly negative – they could ask the manager of the Hotel Bella Vista if they have any bedrooms which are not near wedding parties; they could try and make sure clients don't stay at the hotel on Saturday nights.

B

1 a The report is about 'The Lakes and Julian Alps' holiday. (This is the holiday which featured in Reading A.)
   b The main focus of the report is clients' comments on the accommodation.

2 150 is the more important number because her report is based on the feedback from 150 questionnaires.

3 More than three-quarters were very satisfied.

4 b the picnic lunches at the Turist Hotel (42%)
   c the Hotel Bella Vista
   d breakfast

5 1 Bedrooms at the Turist Hotel
   2 Picnic lunches provided by the Vila Orel and the Turist Hotel
   3 Noise from wedding parties at the Hotel Bella Vista
   4 Remote location of the Turist Hotel

6 a The rooms will be totally redecorated and updated. (In other words …)
   b No, the Vila Orel is prepared to let guests choose their own picnic from the breakfast buffet, but the Turist Hotel isn't. (… whereas …)
   c They might stop offering pre-payment because they are going to suggest that guests arrange their own lunches. (As a result …)

   d They should warn them because most guests stay at the hotel on Saturday night and that is when the weddings take place. (Since …)
   e No, she doesn't because there is a frequent bus service. (However …)

7 *Your own answer. Possible answer:*
Ivana's boss will probably be pleased about the feedback. The majority of clients who have given their comments are very satisfied with the holiday. In addition, Ivana has made some good suggestions for dealing with clients' criticisms.

Focus on linking words

However
a Furthermore / In addition
b For example / For instance
c Furthermore / In addition
d In other words

Unit 12

A

1 b

2 b In the Mail Order department of The International Book Shop.
   c Handle orders, keep the database up-to-date and carry out general tasks related to customer orders.
   d 20 hours a week
   e 1 pm
   f The advert doesn't mention pay.

3 *Your own answers.*

4 b 4   c 2   d 5   e 3

5 You apply by sending in your CV to the Manager of The International Book Shop. You must apply before Wednesday 2nd August.

6 *Your own answer. Possible answer:*
Yes, I think Pilar is suitable for the job. She has experience in sales, in office administration, and in working with people (as a tour guide). In addition, she speaks three languages.

7 *Your own answer. Possible answer:*
I would rather work on the shop floor than in the Mail Order department.

B

1 b salary   c completion   d leave   e proposed
   f Yours sincerely

2 c

3 b position   c is subject to   d in excess of
   e commencement

4 *Possible answers*:
  b to repeat our offer in writing
  c £8,000 a year
  d a 13-week trial period at the start of a new job when you are watched and tested to see if you are suitable for the job
  e how much holiday you are allowed each year
  f 22 days' holiday in a period of 12 months (not always January to December) for which a business plans its management of money (in this case, it actually means 22 mornings' holiday)
  g the longer you work, the more holiday you will get
  h the amount of money you are paid for work
5 Pilar has to write a letter of acceptance, stating when she is available to start work.

Focus on the layout of letters

b F c T d T e F f T g T h F

Pilar's letter of acceptance should look like this:

> 76 Cork Place
> Dublin 7
>
> Mr Michael O'Grady
> The International Book Shop
> 23–25 Meath Road
> Dublin 4
>
> 16 August 20__
>
> Dear Mr O'Grady
>
> Re: Part-time Administrator
>
> Thank you for your offer of employment as Part-time Administrator, which I am delighted to accept.
>
> My proposed commencement date is Monday 3 September. I would like to also add that I have booked a holiday for the last week in October, so I will be unable to work during this period. I hope this will not be inconvenient.
>
> Yours sincerely
>
> *Pilar Morientes*
>
> Pilar Morientes

Unit 13

Get ready to read
○ b 1 c 6 d 3 e 2 f 5
○ *Your own answers.*

A

1 Tables a and b mention GDP.
2 b T c T d F (just <u>over</u> 9 billion US dollars) e T
  f F (contributed <u>less</u> to GDP than business services)
  g F (was <u>three times</u> that of the construction and utilities sector)

3 b third c US d over
4 e line graph f bar chart g pie chart
5 b rose c fewer … than d food
  e about the same amount from China as

B

1 *Your own answers.*
2 b Y c N d N e N
3 a Jackets do not normally have to be worn at meetings because of Singapore's hot and humid weather.
  b Make sure you arrive punctually for business meetings. This is a matter of respect.
  c Your Singaporean counterparts may not greet you with 'Good morning / afternoon / evening' or 'How are you?' Instead, you may be asked 'Have you eaten?' or 'Where are you going?'
  d Handshaking isn't part of Asian culture, so a handshake in Singapore is much softer and lighter to the touch than a Western one.
  e As a sign of respect, Singaporeans don't always look people in the eye – especially if the person is older or has a higher status.
4 a 2 b 1 c 4 d 3
5 *Your own answers.*
6 b 4 c 6 d 7 e 11
7 *Your own answers. Possible answer*:
  In Spain, we are always polite, professional and respectful. Punctuality is also important. There are some differences between Spanish and Singaporean etiquette, however. Meetings can be set up without much notice. Handshaking is very important. Business cards are exchanged at the end of the meeting. Spanish businessmen generally wear jackets all the time because air conditioning can make offices quite cool. There is no informal conversation before a meeting. Respect is shown towards the boss – who is not necessarily the oldest person – but everyone is encouraged to offer their own ideas.

Focus on the passive infinitive

b be made
c be arranged
Examples from text:
point 4: to be seated, point 7: be treated, point 8: be asked, point 9: be worn, point 11: be offended
d be embarrassed
e be told
f be invited
g be introduced
h be greeted
i be expected

Unit 14

Get ready to read

- ⊙ a an encyclopaedia
  b a dictionary
  c a thesaurus
- ⊙ b dictionary of slang
  c dictionary of quotations
  d bilingual dictionary
  e monolingual dictionary

A

1 b 4 c 1 d 2
2 b BRANCH LINE – BREAK
  c GRIPS – GUM
  d LAUD – LAUSANNE
3 a disciple, adherent, partisan, pupil, supporter, enthusiast, devotee, fan, servant, attendant, companion
  b trumpet, trombone
  c be thin on the ground
  d Stan, Oliver
4 b 4 c 1 d 3 e a film guide

Focus on pronunciation

laɪkrə, metəl

5

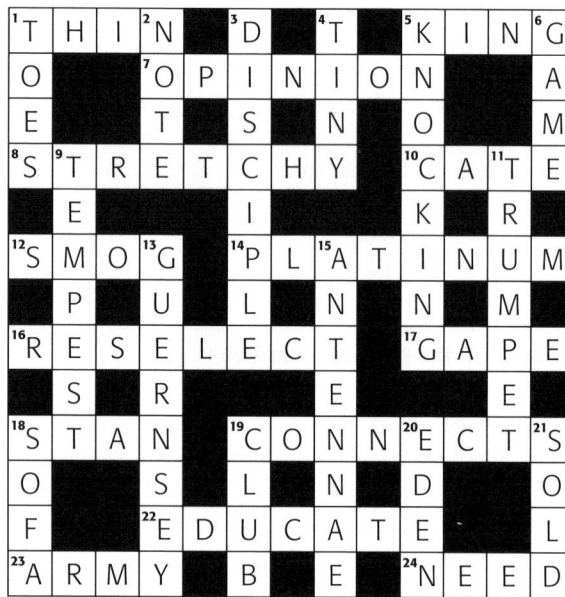

B

1 Don't check your answers yet. You're going to look them up in extracts from a book of facts.
2 You can't be sure which section of the book the answers will be in. You need to find out what the headings are in each section (see Exercise 3). The following answers are possible at this stage of your research.

b Nations of the World / Communication / Arts and Culture
c Communication
d Nations of the World / History
e Nations of the World / Communication
f Nations of the World / History / Science and Technology
g Sports and Games
h Communication / Arts and Culture
i Human Body, Health and Nutrition
j Communication
k Space
l Communication / Arts and Culture

3 The answers to questions a, b, c, e, h, j and l are all in Communication.
b Differences between British and US English
c Some common similes
e Car index marks – international
h Symbols in general use
j Abbreviations and acronyms used in text messages
l Common abbreviations
4 b fall c as blind as a bat e Philippines
h et cetera j Face to face
l répondez s'il vous plaît (please reply)
5 *Your own answer. Possible answer:*
I didn't know that aubergine and eggplant were the same thing. I didn't know that the dollar symbol was used for other currencies.

Extra practice

The answers given in the *Chambers Book of Facts* for the other questions are:
d 1989
f 1937
g Uruguay
i the bone in the lower part of your leg
k Sirius A

Unit 15

Get ready to read

- ⊙ *Your own answers.*
- ⊙ *Your own answers.*
- ⊙ *Your own answers.*

A

2 The catalogue does a, c and d. It also lists all the DVDs, videos, audio books, language courses, printed music, recorded music, etc. which libraries in Oxfordshire hold.
3 a 7 b 10 c 100 d 3
4 c
5 b N c Y d N
6 You should try entering more keywords.

7 *Your own answers. Possible answers*:
  b football Ronaldinho
  c Remains of the Day
  d how to play backgammon
  e history classical music Goodall
  f reading skills
8 two ways
  'Library staff can help you find the right number, or, if you know of another book on the same subject, you can see what class number it has been given, and use that number in your search.'
9 *Your own answers. Possible answers*:
  I might look for a guidebook to Oxford because that would be useful. I'd also look for books for foreign students, especially books about the FCE exam.

B

1 a The book is by Agatha Christie.
  b It's about a murder on a train.
  c Yes. (The back cover mentions the cast, which means the actors in the film version of the book.)
3 a She wrote 80 crime novels and 19 plays.
  b Her books have been translated into 100 languages.
  c More than two billion of her books have been sold in total. (One billion in English, and one billion in other languages.)
4 It is from near the beginning of the story.
5 Mrs McGillicuddy's first name is Elspeth.
6 The following parts of the text show that the ticket collector doesn't think she is telling the truth:
  The ticket collector looked at her doubtfully.
  'I beg your pardon, madam?'

  The ticket collector looked extremely doubtful.
  'Strangled?' he said disbelievingly.

  'You don't think, madam, that you may have had a little nap and – er –'

  'Now don't you think, madam, that you'd been reading an exciting story, and that you just dropped off, and awaking a little confused –'

  The ticket collector sighed reluctantly …

  The ticket collector looked as though he thought Mrs McGillicuddy was quite capable of seeing anything anywhere as the fancy took her.
7 *Your own answer. Possible answer*:
  Yes, I think I would be interested in reading this book. It has lots of direct speech, so it seems quite easy to follow. I also like crime fiction in general.

Focus on adverbs

a The ticket collector looked at her doubtfully.
b 'Strangled?' he said disbelievingly.
c coughed apologetically   d broke off tactfully
e said persuasively   f sighed reluctantly
h apologetically   i reluctantly   j persuasively
k tactfully   l doubtfully

Unit 16

Get ready to read

◉ *Your own answers.*
◉ *Your own answers. Possible answers*:
  Reading is very important – it's the way we find out and learn things. Almost everything I know in English, for example, I know because I read it. We read books, newspapers, magazines, etc. We also read lots of other kinds of things – tickets, labels, vouchers, recipes, adverts, road signs. I don't know exactly how we read – it's something to do with the eye jumping along the line of text rather than looking at each word individually.
◉ *Your own answer. Possible answer*:
  I hope they will!

A

1 *Your own answers.*
2 It is from paragraph a.
3 The most important points are in the first sentences of each paragraph:
  1 People differ in reading ability.
  2 A good reader uses various reading techniques.
  3 Reading can be classified into three main kinds: (1) recreational reading, (2) study-type reading, and (3) survey reading.
  4 Recreational reading can provide hour after hour of enjoyment.
  5 Study-type reading usually requires the reader to pay close attention to the text.
  6 Survey reading involves covering a large amount of text to get a general idea of its content.
  7 Shifting among kinds of reading. Most people use different reading techniques for different reading situations.
  8 Good readers can easily shift from one kind of reading to another.
  9 Reading flexibility improves with experience.
4 *Your own answer. Possible answer*:
  Nothing is completely new to me. I'm a little surprised that the text doesn't mention scanning – reading quickly to find a specific piece of information. I suppose this comes under survey reading – you look quickly and decide if a text is likely to give you the specific information, and then you identify the piece of information you want.

5 *Your own answers.*
You will probably agree that you have used survey reading and then study-type reading.

6 b types of text
c like
d link the main ideas together
e only some parts
f they know

7 *Your own answer. Possible answer:*
I think it describes what I do in my own language. But I'd like to be more flexible in my approach to reading English and be more confident. I don't need to read word by word.

8 *Your own answer. Possible answer:*
I'd tell them to try and read with a clear purpose in mind so that they know what they want to get out of the text. I'd tell them to try and distinguish between texts which need to be read word by word and texts which can be surveyed. Once you've found what you need to know in a text you're surveying, you don't need to read the rest.

B

1 a 2 b 1 c 3
2 Topic a paragraphs 4, 5 and 6
Topic b paragraphs 1 and 2
Topic c paragraphs 7 and 8
3 e
4 b T c F d T e T
5 *Your own answer. Possible answer:*
I used structural analysis with *misunderstandings* – it has the prefix *mis* (= not/badly), the root *understand*, the ending *ing*. It also comes after *correct*, so it is a noun – also it has an *s* ending. I think it means 'something you have understood wrongly'.
6 *Your own answer. Possible answer:*
I read a friend's dissertation in Turkish (my language), but I hardly understood any of it. His subject was chemistry, and mine was history. I lacked the background.
7 *Your own answer. Possible answer:*
I'd tell them to read as much as they could. That will help their verbal memory, and help them to practise working out the meaning of unknown words.

Focus on prefixes and suffixes

b unaware   c selection   d information
e misunderstandings   f knowledge
h awareness   i selective   j informer/informant
k understandable   l knowledgeable

Review2

A 1 T 2 F 3 T 4 T 5 T 6 F 7 T 8 F
C 9 a non-fiction book
10 an email
11 a novel
12 a webpage
D 13 a 14 c 15 b 16 a 17 b
E 18 ✗ 19 ✗ 20 ✗ 21 ✓ 22 ✓
F 23 a 24 b 25 d 26 g 27 i
G 28 2004
29 less than
30 more than
31 two
32 dropped a position
H 33 b
34 c
I 35 carpeting, floorboards, tiles
36 cracked, loose, crumbling
37 an object that is in the way
38 boxes, rubbish bins
39 obvious
40 spill(s), puddle, moisture
41 adaptor
42 in working order
J *Your own answers. Possible answers:*
43 You might slip on an icy surface.
44 You might trip over an electrical lead if it isn't close to a wall.
45 You might fall over boxes on the stairs.
K 46 no
47 no
48 yes
49 yes
L 50 states
51 ensure
52 nominate
53 record
54 encounter
55 inform

Real skills for real life

A brand new, four-level skills series

For photocopiable skills activities, try these Copy Collection titles…

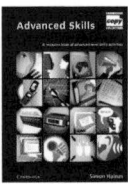
Book & Audio CD
978-0-521-60848-0

Book
978-0-521-53287-7

Book
978-0-521-53405-5

Book
978-0-521-60582-3

Book & Audio CDs (2)
978-0-521-75461-3

Book & Audio CD
978-0-521-75464-4

Book
978-0-521-55981-2
Cassette
978-0-521-55980-5

Book
978-0-521-55979-9
Cassette
978-0-521-55978-2

Book
978-0-521-62612-5
Cassettes
978-0-521-62611-8

Please order through your usual bookseller.
In case of difficulty, please contact:

ELT Marketing, Cambridge University Press, The Edinburgh Building, Cambridge, CB2 8RU, UK

Tel: +44 (0)1223 325922
Fax: +44 (0)1223 325984

Listening & Speaking

Level 1	Level 2	Level 3	Level 4

With answers & Audio CDs (2) 978-0-521-70198-3	With answers & Audio CDs (2) 978-0-521-70200-3	With answers & Audio CDs (2) 978-0-521-70588-2	With answers & Audio CDs (2) 978-0-521-70590-5
Without answers 978-0-521-70199-0	Without answers 978-0-521-70201-0	Without answers 978-0-521-70589-9	Without answers 978-0-521-70591-2

Writing

Level 1	Level 2	Level 3	Level 4

With answers & Audio CD 978-0-521-70184-6	With answers & Audio CD 978-0-521-70186-0	With answers & Audio CD 978-0-521-70592-9	With answers & Audio CD 978-0-521-70594-3
Without answers 978-0-521-70185-3	Without answers 978-0-521-70187-7	Without answers 978-0-521-70593-6	Without answers 978-0-521-70595-0

Reading

Level 1	Level 2	Level 3	Level 4

With answers 978-0-521-70202-7	With answers 978-0-521-70204-1	With answers 978-0-521-70573-8	With answers 978-0-521-70575-2
Without answers 978-0-521-70203-4	Without answers 978-0-521-70205-8	Without answers 978-0-521-70574-5	Without answers 978-0-521-70576-9

Bring your skills to life

For teacher's notes, visit: **www.cambridge.org/englishskills**